Social Work in Post-War and Political Conflict Areas

Kristin Sonnenberg · Cinur Ghaderi
Editors

Social Work in Post-War and Political Conflict Areas

Examples from Iraqi-Kurdistan and beyond

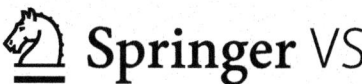

Editors
Kristin Sonnenberg
Protestant University of Applied Sciences
Bochum, Germany

Cinur Ghaderi
Protestant University of Applied Sciences
Bochum, Germany

ISBN 978-3-658-32059-1   ISBN 978-3-658-32060-7 (eBook)
https://doi.org/10.1007/978-3-658-32060-7

© The Editor(s) (if applicable) and The Author(s), under exclusive license to Springer Fachmedien Wiesbaden GmbH, part of Springer Nature 2021
This work is subject to copyright. All rights are solely and exclusively licensed by the Publisher, whether the whole or part of the material is concerned, specifically the rights of translation, reprinting, reuse of illustrations, recitation, broadcasting, reproduction on microfilms or in any other physical way, and transmission or information storage and retrieval, electronic adaptation, computer software, or by similar or dissimilar methodology now known or hereafter developed.
The use of general descriptive names, registered names, trademarks, service marks, etc. in this publication does not imply, even in the absence of a specific statement, that such names are exempt from the relevant protective laws and regulations and therefore free for general use.
The publisher, the authors and the editors are safe to assume that the advice and information in this book are believed to be true and accurate at the date of publication. Neither the publisher nor the authors or the editors give a warranty, expressed or implied, with respect to the material contained herein or for any errors or omissions that may have been made. The publisher remains neutral with regard to jurisdictional claims in published maps and institutional affiliations.

This Springer VS imprint is published by the registered company Springer Fachmedien Wiesbaden GmbH part of Springer Nature.
The registered company address is: Abraham-Lincoln-Str. 46, 65189 Wiesbaden, Germany

Preface

Behind us lies a very special time of cooperation, which began in 2015. We are grateful that we have gone down this path together with colleagues, friends and families.

We would like to thank the authors represented in this book for their willingness to revise their presentations from the international conference in October 2019 once again for the manuscript. The result is a wonderful composition of topics and perspectives.

The conference would not have been possible without our partners from the University of Sulaimani and the NGO HAUKARI e.V. As a representative of this institution, we would especially like to thank Karin Mlodoch, for her fantastic cooperation over the years.

So many things we could never have realized on our own: Most of all we would like to thank our families in different roles: Kamil, Mina, Milian, Volker, Lotte und Johanna. You supported us with networks, your special translation skills, delicious food and technical know-how. And you gave us emotional support and space to work on the project.

In the end it was our English editor who actively supported us in the realization of this book project. Therefore, special thanks goes to Dr. Sania Jardine for her thorough and reflective accompaniment of our texts. Her cautiously critical and meticulous queries have added to the precision of the texts in many places that we would not have been able to achieve as a non-native speakers. We would like to thank our student assistant Marie Müller-Handrejk, who has always supported us reliably, flexibly and very thoroughly in checking English texts and editing the final layout.

Kristin Sonnenberg
Cinur Ghaderi

Contents

Framing the Topic—A Multi-Dimensional Approach to Social Work in Post-War and Political Conflict Areas 1
Cinur Ghaderi and Kristin Sonnenberg

Social Work, Armed Conflict and Post-War Reconstruction 25
Ruth Seifert

International Social Work and the Global Social Work Statement of Ethical Principles 45
Kristin Sonnenberg

Knowledge Production in International Social Work – Postcolonial Perspectives 65
Nausikaa Schirilla

There Are Many Roads to a School of Social Work. Importance of the International for Modern Social Work 73
Rebekka Ehret

Systematising Local Knowledge: Hierarchies, Power Relations and Decontextualisation in West–East Knowledge Transfer 91
Karin Mlodoch

Community-Based Psychosocial Work to Change the Cycle of Violence in Post Conflict Areas 111
Berenice Meintjes

**Children Born of Wartime Rapes – an Analysis
from a Gender-Sensitive and Psychosocial Perspective** 125
Cinur Ghaderi

**The Refugee as a Stigmatized Individual – Spoiled Identities,
Possible Causes and Courses of Action for Social Work** 143
Lisa-Marie Dünnebacke and Kristin Goetze

Contributors

Kristin Sonnenberg, Prof. Dr. Professor of Social Work at the Protestant University of Applied Sciences Bochum. She studied Social Pedagogy in Germany, finished an MA in Comparative European Social Studies at the University of North London and her PhD at the University of Cologne in Germany 2004 at the faculty of Educational Science. She is a qualified Psychodrama trainer. Since 2011 she is specialized in the field of methods and conceptualizing social work. Her main research projects are social inclusion of people with disabilities and international social work. She is member of the German Association of Social Workers (DGSA). Since 2016 she is head of the BA Social Work Studies and together with Prof. Ghaderi she was leader of the DAAD-cooperation project CoBoSUnin 2016-2019 between the University of Sulaimani and EvH Bochum. Contact: sonnenberg@evh-bochum.de

Cinur Ghaderi, Prof. Dr. Professor of psychology within the faculty of social work at the Protestant University of Applied Sciences (EvH RWL Bochum). She is Vice-President for Research, Transfer and Internalization. After her postgraduate education in psychological psychotherapy (behavioral therapy), she worked in the "Psychosocial Centre for refugees" (PSZ) in Düsseldorf. She received her PhD at the faculty of Social Sciences at Ruhr-Universität-Bochum. She is a member of the steering committee of dtppp (transcultural psychiatry, psychotherapy and psychosomatics). Main academic interests: International Social Work, Refugee Studies, Transcultural Psychotherapy, Psychotrauma, Identity, Diversity and Gender. She is the initiator of the DAAD-cooperation project CoBoSUnin 2016-2019 between the University of Sulaimani and EvH Bochum. Contact: ghaderi@evh-bochum.de

Ruth Seifert, Prof. Dr. University of Applied Sciences Regensburg, Germany/Dept. of Ap-plied Social and Health Sciences. She studied social sciences, philosophy and American Studies in Munich and Philadelphia, Pa./USA. She worked in various research projects and ten years in academic and research institutions of the German Armed Forces before be-coming Prof. of Sociology at the University of Applied Sciences in Regensburg in 1999. Areas of research and publication: internation-al social work, sexualized violence and armed conflicts, gender and the military, gender and post-conflict reconstruction, theories of inclusion and exclusion. 2005-2012 head of a DAAD-cooperation project that established a new Department of Social Work at the University of Prishtina/Kosovo. Since 2012 Erasmus cooperation with that department and the University of Applied Sciences, Regensburg. Contact: ruth-seifert@t-online

Nausikaa Schirilla, Prof. Dr. MA in philosophy, PhD and habilitation in educational sciences Goethe University Frankfurt/Main, working experience in political education, adult education and social work in Frankfurt/Main, since 2005 Prof. for Social Work, migration and cross-cultural competence, Catholic University of Applied Sciences, Freiburg, Germany. Contact: nausikaa.schirilla@kh-freiburg.de

Rebekka Ehret, Dr. she is a Social Anthropologist and a Sociolinguist. Before her position as a lecturer and researcher at the Institute of Socio-Cultural Development at the University of Applied Sciences and Arts in Lucerne, Switzerland, she held the same position at the Institute of Social Anthropology at the University of Basel, Switzerland. Between 2004 and 2008 she worked for the UN at the Special Court for Sierra Leone and at the Extraordinary Chambers to the Courts of Cambodia. Her field of expertise is language and identity, creolization, migration, intersectionality and transcategorial communication, She is a member of the steering committee of dtppp (transcultural psychiatry, psychotherapy and psychosomatics). Contact: rebekka.ehret@hslu.ch

Karin Mlodoch, Prof. Dr. is a psychologist. She holds a PhD from the Institute of Social Psy-chology, Ethnopsychoanalysis and Psychotraumatology at the University of Klagenfurt/Austria and is an assistant professor at the Sigmund Freud University Berlin. She is a founding and board member of the German based NGO HAUKARI - Association for International Cooperation, which supports humanitarian aid and development projects in the Kurdistan Region of Iraq and Iraq with a focus on support for women survivors of political, social and gender-based violence and women and youth empowerment. Main fields of research and practices: socio-political perspectives on trauma; memory research;

intercultural psychosocial work; international development policies: Contact: mlodoch@haukari.de

Berenice Meintjes is a clinical psychologist who has been involved in community-based peace-building and trauma work in KwaZulu-Natal South Africa. She has had the privilege of being involved in training, moni-toring and evaluation initiatives in several African countries, includ-ing Mozambique, Tanzania, Sierra Leone and Zimbabwe, and also in the Kurdistan Region of Iraq and in Kosovo. Berenice is a strong advocate for strengthening locally appropriate responses to adversity. One of her latest interests is supporting sur-vivor and other social justice movements to collectively address their advocacy concerns. Publications: See www.survivors.org.za and www.repssi.org; Contact: bearpsv@iafrica.com

Lisa-Marie Dünnebacke, M.A., B.A. German philology/comparative education' (2010); M.A. ‚Social inclusion' (2014). From 02/2017-12/2019 scientific asso-ciate and lecturer at EvH, Bochum, freelance Social Justice- & Diversity trainer and since 01/2020 head of education in the child and youth service Martinswerk e.V. Dorlar, Schmallenberg HSK; among that preparation of PhD-thesis [projec-ted thematic focal point: masculinity constructions in Kurdistan-Iraq]; Contact: l.duennebacke@outlook.com

Kristin Goetze, M.A. Diploma ‚Social Work'(2012); M.A. ‚Management in social institutions' (2015). Since 09/2014 lecturer at the faculty of Social Work, Müns-ter and EvH Bochum and since 09/2016 research assistant at the faculty of social work at the EvH, Bochum; since 05/2017 PhD-student at the University of Ham-burg about coping strategies of refugees in dealing with social exclusion; Contact: goetze@fh-muenster.de

Framing the Topic—A Multi-Dimensional Approach to Social Work in Post-War and Political Conflict Areas

Cinur Ghaderi and Kristin Sonnenberg

Abstract

This book offers a unique approach to theoretical concepts and practical examples around the topic of international social work in the context of war and conflicts. The reader gains knowledge about the competences and the role of social work, which contribute to mitigating the effects of war and conflict. The book raises the question how to connect international social work with local approaches and offers suggestions for a development of social work with a view to exchanging knowledge and experience between the so-called Global North and Global South, the West and the East. The role of social work in reducing the problem of gender-based violence and the methods of peacebuilding processes in post-war and post-conflict societies are also discussed.

Keywords

Social work · War · Conflict · International · Post-colonial theory · International social work

---

C. Ghaderi (✉) · K. Sonnenberg
Protestant University of Applied Sciences, Bochum, Deutschland
E-Mail: ghaderi@evh-bochum.de

K. Sonnenberg
E-Mail: sonnenberg@evh-bochum.de

© The Author(s), under exclusive license to Springer Fachmedien Wiesbaden GmbH, part of Springer Nature 2021
K. Sonnenberg and C. Ghaderi (eds.), *Social Work in Post-War and Political Conflict Areas*, https://doi.org/10.1007/978-3-658-32060-7_1

1 Introduction

This book focuses on social work in post-war and conflict regions. In this introduction, the topic is embedded in five contexts and explained accordingly: 1) as part of an international discourse on social work in war and crisis regions in general, and specifically as a result of an international conference which took place in Slemani, Kurdistan-Iraq, at the end of October 2019 to mark the conclusion of a binational project, 2) as a theoretical and practical field of intervention of social work, 3) as a critical contribution to knowledge production from a post-colonial perspective on international social work, 4) as a product of local experience in the pioneering phase of social work in the Kurdistan Region of Iraq, and finally 5) based on concrete themes like community-based psychosocial work, children born of wartime rapes and refugees as stigmatized individuals.

This volume is also part of a collection of several publications and a multilingual film:

1. A documentary film presents the international cooperation project between the Departments of Social Work at the Protestant University of Applied Sciences in Bochum (EvH) and the University of Sulaimani (UoS). It provides an insight into social work in Kurdistan-Iraq and Germany, for example in the areas of migration and flight, gender and violence, and international social work. In the second part, the film shows excerpts from the International Conference.[1]
2. In addition, a first textbook, *Introduction to Social Work*, in Kurdish-Sorani is published, in which the majority of the authors are lecturers from the Faculty of Social Work at the University of Sulaimani. The aim is to promote the development of indigenous teaching materials and research in accordance with local communities and their conditions. The book will be published simultaneously in 2021.
3. A joint editorial volume (in English) on the topic of *Social Work at the Level of International Comparison: Examples from Iraqi-Kurdistan and Germany* will be prepared by the CoBoSUnin[2] project team. This volume, which will be also published in 2021, will present the results of the project, with about 40 contributions from both participating countries.

---

[1] A documentation about the CoBoSUnin-project. The film offers insights into social work in Kurdistan Region of Iraq and Germany. A Film by Ernst Meyer, SMIDAK Filmproduktion, Berlin: https://www.youtube.com/watch?v=wEkW9v51fps.

[2] CoBoSUnin = Cooperation between Bochum and Sulaimania Universities nowadays.

4. This volume, the third book in this collection, places a special focus on social work in war and crisis regions.
5. A number of conference articles, written in Kurdish or Arabic, will be published in a special edition of the UoS Journal.

It should be noted that the original plan was to publish all contributions jointly in three languages, which turned out not to be practicable. The international dialogue, however, will continue.

Explanation about the naming 'Slemani'
After a long reflection of the different versions and possibilities to write the name of the town, where the University of Sulaimani is placed, we decided to use the Kurdish version *Slemani* in our texts. We think with regard to de-colonizing processes and the empowerment of people concerned, it is the best solution, to take the version, the citizens themselves use and not an English or Arabic or German interpretation. Within our research we found the following versions:

Anglophone texts:

1. Sulaimaniya
2. Sulaimaniyah
3. Sulaymaniyah
4. Sulaymaniyyah

Other versions:

5. Sulaimania (German language, English texts of NGOs, e.g. Haukari)
6. As- Sulaymaniyyah (Arabic pronunciation, Arabic authors using English language)

The justification for this decision is not essentialist in the sense that the real, original Kurdish version would be called. For this would indeed be a classic 'identity trap' (Sen 2007) that ignores the historical interactions and is oriented towards singular reduced explanations. The city of Slemani was founded in 1784 by Ibrahim Pashai Baban. He named the city 'Sleman Pasha' after his father, with the aim of establishing a capital of the Kurdish principality of Baban. The name Sleman comes from Arabic, is probably derived from Salam and means peace. The variants of this name alone fill an entire Wikipedia page (https://de.wikipedia.org/wiki/Suleiman). The Arabic name Sleman in turn is related or a derivation of the name 'Solomon' comes from Hebrew, from which the word 'shalom' (peace) is also derived. Solomon was the son of David in the Old Testament, and according to biblical reports, he was the builder of the first Jewish temple in Jerusalem and the third king in Israel. These brief notes should suffice to make it clear that '(…) the decolonization of the Spirit requires that we say goodbye to the temptation of exclusive identities.' (ibid, p. 111).

2 Embedding the Topic as the Subject of an International Conference

The contributions in this publication are based on papers presented at an international conference on *Social Work in Post-War and Political Conflict Areas* in October 2019 in Kurdistan-Iraq,[3] hosted by the University of Sulaimani. International experts, academics and practitioners from Kurdistan, the Middle East, Europe and South Africa came together to discuss the challenges of social work, and of dealing with the effects of wars and conflicts.

With the contribution and support of interpreters (Arabic-English-Kurdish) an academic exchange was made possible, concerning five topics: *International Social Work, International Comparison, Gender and Violence, Strengthening Social Work to Meet the Needs of Communities* and *The Future of Social Work in Kurdistan*.

The conference formed part of the international project ‚*CoBoSUnin*—Cooperation between Bochum and Sulaimani Universities nowadays', a cooperation between the faculties of Social Work at the Protestant University of Applied Sciences in Bochum, Germany, and the University of Sulaimani in the Kurdistan Region of Iraq. The four-year university project, which ran from 2016 to 2019, was financed by the German Academic Exchange Service with funding from the Federal Foreign Office. The *CoBoSUnin* project aimed to strengthen the internationalization of teaching and research in the field of social work at both universities.[4] The goal was not only to promote the knowledge society in Kurdistan-Iraq in the context of a sustainable development policy, but also

---

[3]Conference report in *German*: https://www.evh-bochum.de/artikel/konferenz-cobosunin-team-schliesst-kooperation-ab.html; *Kurdish*: https://univsul.edu.iq/en/news/1968/34---u-u and https://univsul.edu.iq/en/event/1965/34; *English*: https://www.haukari.de/files/pdf/HAUKARI_KHANZAD_Invitation_Conference_SocialWorkOctober2019.pdf.

[4]cf. project description: https://www.evh-bochum.de/files/Dateiablage/transfer/laufende_TP/Transfer_laufende_DP_CoBoSUnin.pdf.

to reflect critically on the local and global knowledge production of international social work and to contribute to the internationalization and transcultural knowledge dialogue of both universities.

Other partners were involved in the implementation of the International Conference, like the German aid organisations HAUKARI e. V. and the women's center KHANZAD in Slemani. These collaborations were important because the organizations had experience in transnational cooperation as well as in the practice of social work in Kurdistan. As a result, they were familiar with critical aspects of the local society, such as social work in cases of gender-based violence and psychosocial work with refugees.

The international conference provided a platform for discussing an important topic of social work, bringing together scientific theory, research and practice as well as local and international knowledge. Over 400 delegates attended the conference. This impressive number showed that the conference topic, 'Social Work in Post-War and Political Conflict Areas' had struck a chord with many stakeholders. The venue, Slemani in the Kurdistan Region of Iraq, has a history of multiple wars and can still be described as a conflicted area. In autumn 2019, at the same time as the conference took place, events and political conflicts around Syria and Rojava, the autonomous Kurdish Region in Northern Syria, affected the Kurdistan Region in Syria. International media coverage and concern for the people of Syria and Rojava were ever-present topics.

Social work requires professionalism, and this includes being aware of its political dimension as a human rights profession. There are different levels of politics in social work: dealing with the addressees through public relations, through professional associations and the interlocking of these levels. An exchange on these questions is interesting: How political should social work be? How political should science be? How might social work mitigate the effects of war and conflict? How can local and international approaches be connected? The conference provided a space for listening and understanding whether and how social work works in different contexts, which concepts it uses, and what critical and emancipatory concepts inform it.

3   Embedding the Topic as a Theoretical and Practical Field of Intervention in an International Context

Armed conflicts and wars cause suffering, destruction and human rights violations. A profession that sees itself as a human rights profession is asked to politicize the suffering of individuals on the basis of its professional standards. It has to take on an international perspective, since the misery resulting from armed conflicts and wars is not evenly distributed globally, but the profession is intertwined in the causes and effects of this suffering.

When is a war a war? Definitions of war have changed, as have the wars themselves. In literature, a distinction is made between old and new wars. Seifert, with reference to Kaldor and Münkler, states:

> 'Roughly summarized, *new war* theories claim that *old wars* took place between nation states primarily of the Northern hemisphere, were of a geo-political and/or ideological nature, often based on grievances whereas *new wars* are wars located in countries of the South, are mostly identity-based, i.e. power claims are based on allegedly traditional identities, e.g. ethno-national or tribal belonging or religion.' (Seifert 2018, p. 185).

After the Second World War, the concept of international armed conflicts was introduced, which refers to the intergovernmental use of armed force and can be distinguished from micro-conflicts and incidents in the intensity of hostility. War is classified as a subcategory of armed conflicts (Dülffer 2016). The category of internal armed conflicts is used for civil wars and national liberation movements, where the actors involved are not subjects of humanitarian international law. This area, however, falls within the scope of international human rights and related violations (BMVG 2019, p. 10).

Common to all definitions and practices is the systematic use of force over an extended period of time and the lethal use of weapons. Two or more organized groups carry out armed clashes.

> 'The classical definition of war assumes that at least one of the two actors is a state (…). The aim is to assert its own superiority by means of an attack, intervention, sanctions, defence and liberation war and to defeat the opponent. At the same time the opponents are killed or injured and the infrastructure and (natural) livelihoods are severely damaged. The cause is usually economic or ideological.' (Federal Centre for Political Education, Security Policy[5]).

Objects of conflict range from ideological-systemic, national, or territorial domination to power over resources or decolonization and autonomy.

In this book we deliberately talk about post-war and political conflict areas. For nowadays, the once clearly separated social conditions of war and peace seem to intertwine. Domestic conflicts, terrorism, cyber attacks and tactics such as propaganda and disinformation, as well as the diversity of the actors involved,

---

[5]translated by the authors.

call into question the traditional image of war. Düllfer speaks of *unconventional, asymmetrical, new* and *hybrid* wars (Düllfer 2016).

Depending on the approach, interpretations of when a dispute is a war or a conflict differ. A distinction is made between quantitative approaches, which largely refer to the number of fatalities per year, and qualitative approaches, which classify war according to its characteristics, patterns of cause and effect, and functional logic (BICC 2011).

Thus, the Heidelberg Institute for International Conflict Research (HIIK) describes war as the highest of five levels of conflict, which, like crises, are counted as violent conflicts. If there are 25 to 999 casualties, the Peace Research Institute Oslo (PRIO) speaks of a conflict, and if there are more, the dispute is described as a war (see Violence Conflict according to PRIO/UCDP). Equally, the Correlates of War (COW) approach by David Singer and Melvin Small at the University of Michigan defines an armed conflict with more than 1000 fatalities as a war. On the other hand, the Research Group for Causes of War (AKUF) at the University of Hamburg uses a definition by the Hungarian peace researcher István Kende to describe disputes as conflicts if not all the characteristics of the chosen definition of war are fulfilled.

In addition to the arbitrary use of different numbers of fatalities, it is important to understand that 'neither the social, economic and cultural effects of armed conflicts, nor the victims of, for example, epidemics or famines as a direct consequence of the war-destroyed infrastructure' (BICC) are taken into account in these approaches. The HIIK currently measures the intensity of violence in a conflict using five indicators: 'Type and strength of the weapons used, strength of the personnel employed, number of deaths recorded, number of refugees observed and the extent of the destruction caused by the conflict' (Schwank 2019). It distinguishes five levels of intensity: dispute, non-violent crisis, violent crisis, limited war and war. Violent crisis, limited war and war together form the category 'violent conflicts', in contrast to 'non-violent conflicts' (dispute and non-violent crisis), which are also referred to as *low-intensity conflicts*. Accordingly, violent crises are *medium-intensity conflicts* and wars and limited wars are both *high-intensity conflicts* (HIIK).

In a world characterized by global phenomena such as climate change, urbanization, gender shift, technologization and digitization, the economic divide between North and South, wars, armed conflicts, extreme social asymmetries and massive movements of refugees and migrants, the development of an international perspective on social work is of particular importance. Not least the Corona pandemic has made the global interdependencies of problems and their solutions, and the crystallization of social inequalities along the lines of wealth, gender, and migration, even clearer. The transnational solidarity public, which is involved in wars and extreme situations (e.g. in the case of climate catastrophes, terrorist attacks or the Corona pandemic), implies a transnational community of destiny and a potential concern of all people with a common need. But the world risks (cf. Beck 2007) do not affect all people in the same way, they are often selective, even if the effects interact. The misery of the world is not distributed equally across the globe, as the Human Development Index and the Indices of Social Development regularly show. With respect to conflicts and wars, the analysis shows that '[t]he global political conflict panorama of 2019 was characterized by the continuity of highly violent conflicts, despite a slight decline. Compared to the previous year, the number of wars fell slightly from 16 to 15. While these were held in Africa, America and the Middle East and North Africa (MENA) region, the HIIK did not register any war in Asia and Europe' (HIIK 2020). In 2019, HIIK observed a total of 358 conflicts worldwide. About 55%, 196, were fought violently, while 162 remained on a non-violent level. The number of limited wars decreased from 25 to 23 (ibid.). This high number of conflicts has to be seen in the context of the specific impact on women and children—as evident from the number and strategic use of rape in war, and child soldiers—as well as the number of war tools, small arms and arms exports. When discussing social work in crises, it is also crucial to realize that according to UNHCR, there were almost 80 million refugees in 2019, including 41 million IDPs (Internal Displaced People). This high number of refugees is due to violent conditions such as war, displacement and the living situation in a post-war situation.

Warlike conflicts have an impact on psychological, economic, social and cultural levels. Experiences of violence wound individuals, families and communities. They influence identities, structures and perspectives. Social work as a human rights profession seeks to counteract these effects by healing and supporting, at the individual level and in communities. Important questions to raise are: How can social work contribute to mitigating the effects of war and conflict? What is the role of social work in reducing gender-based-violence? What are the methods of peacebuilding processes in post-war and post-conflict societies?

Involvement in post-war and political-conflict areas is not a classic field of social work, even though the pioneers of social work always had peace in mind whilst fighting against social injustice. Thus Staub-Bernasconi speaks of 'an old and new topic of social work' (2004, p. 9) with reference to the study of the consequences of warfare and its contribution in the international context. Diplomatic efforts after the First World War led to the founding of the International League for Peace and Freedom, a UN-NGO in which social workers were involved, and also the founding of the Save the Children Fund in 1919 (ibid. p. 10). In Germany, the state-run relief system was extended for war widows, war orphans and war invalids. Due to extensive poverty and unemployment, voluntary benefits were introduced as war-social-welfare at communal level (Engelke et al. 2009, p. 176). Two female pioneers of professional Western social work, Jane Addams (1860–1935) from North America and Alice Salomon (1872–1948) from Germany, are well known for their commitment to peace, democracy and social justice. In 1931, Jane Addams was the first American to receive the Nobel Peace Prize. Alice Salomon, who had a Jewish background, had to leave Germany in 1937, shortly before the outbreak of the Second World War (ibid., p. 238). In 1945, 50 nations founded the United Nations (UN). Their aims are to ensure world peace, protect human rights, create equal rights for all people, and improve the general living standards in the world. The Universal Declaration of Human Rights from 1948 and its updates form the basis of the Ethics of Social Work—Principles and Standards (ibid., p. 331 and contribution→ *Kristin Sonnenberg* in this book). Throughout its history of professionalization, social work in the second half of the twentieth century has a broad theoretical base and varied points of reference. Some of these are unpolitical and focus on curative-therapeutic approaches and individual contexts. Others, especially in connection with social movements (youth, women, anti-psychiatry), are more critical towards the system and power inequalities. Examples are radical approaches, anti-oppressive social work, empowering concepts or theories deriving from system theory. At the end of the twentieth century and the beginning of the twenty-first century, there has been a shift towards managerialism and neoliberal ideas with profit orientation and free markets (Sonnenberg 2004, pp. 17). A new, more political shift can be observed in ecological approaches and a focus on global responsibilities in the context of the UN Millennium development goals and social movements like Fridays for Future. Within the academic discourse, one example would be the book 'Green Social Work—From Environmental Crises to Environmental Justice' by Lena Dominelli (2016), where she discusses the role of social work as part of an integrated socio-ecological debate and combines ideas of social and environmental justice.

In practice, it would be hard to identify social work activities that have no social and power-political implications (Gore 1968, p. 65 quoted after Staub-Bernasconi 2019, p.95). Therefore, the subjects of social work themselves give the mandate for critical and political action without the need for an explicit mandate from politics or society (cf. ibid. pp. 95). Critical social work is capable of criticism and political engagement due to an ethical and cognitive distance from political power relations. Professional social work reflects on the conflicts inherent to its role, handles ambivalent loyalties and needs to conduct power-critical analyses if it wants to be political. Staub-Bernasconi argues that the Code of

Ethics itself gives the political mandate to fight against injustice, oppression and the violation of human rights (ibid., p. 96). Sometimes, however, theories and methods to react to the inequalities are still missing at concrete levels, which, according to Staub-Bernasconi, makes it even more important to develop approaches and make the topic visible in the context of conflicts and war. She assumes that power structures can only be changed by altering social rules and norms applied by the individuals or within society (such as in racist neighbourhoods, patriarchal family structures or violence in communities or districts). It is central to restore the dignity of individuals, to empower the people concerned and assist them to realise legitimate rights against illegitimate structures. In this volume, the contributions by *Karin Mlodoch* and *Berenice Meintjes* give examples of critical and empowering strategies.

In the history of social work, the history of aid, conflict reduction and the boundaries of politics are always closely linked. The example of the tasks and roles of international NGOs shows that they are potentially controversial and that their mandate reflects a classic ambivalence of social work in the sense of the double mandate[6] of aid and control (cf. McMahon 2019). On the one hand, NGOs offer frontline services and are providing a great deal of humanitarian assistance at a local level. They are promoting economic development and human rights, and are the 'moving element of thoughtful professionals who strive hard to bring about change from the ground up' (ibid. p. 22)—especially since they are confronted with paradoxes and needs that the globalized economy produces. On the other hand, they are part of the 'government from a distance' (Bähr et. al 2014, p. 17),[7] linked to the norms and practices of world politics through financial dependencies and are thus easily influenced. The largest NGOs were founded by Western states and reflect only selected interests of global civil society (McMahon 2019, p. 273). Social work does not, however, want to be a 'social-political rubbish dump of globalisation' (Bähr et al. 2014, p. 13). It faces the challenge of reflecting on the political dimension of the profession again and again. Staub-Bernasconi has introduced this theoretical and ethical perspective as a third mandate in social work, the triple-mandate (2018, pp. 111, 2019, pp. 83).

In post-conflict societies in particular, social work as a political actor can make a professional contribution on several levels: It can support destroyed psyches, family units and solidarity networks, and reinstate access to resources, education,

---

[6]The original idea of the so called double mandate derives from the 1970s, Böhnisch und Lösch 1973.

[7]The original quote, Bähr et al. 2014, p. 17, is: "Einerseits ist sie ein Teil der 'Regierung auf Distanz', anderseits wird sie vor Ort weiterhin und heute vielleicht entschiedener mit den Paradoxien und Bedürftigkeiten konfrontiert, die die globalisierte Ökonomie hervorbringt".

employment and care (for example for orphaned children). It can also revitalize the social infrastructure by supporting schools and youth centres.

In the long term, much more influence is possible: Violent wars and conflicts require legitimacy and ideologies that categorize and dehumanize other people as homogeneous groups in order to normalize the path for the deadly hatred of innocent others. In times of war, a wide variety of cruel forms of violence, used as a means of power, seem to be expected, including gender-based violence through mass rape or enslavement of women, the recruitment of child soldiers or genocides against social and ethnic groups. In the post-war phase, these standards do not disappear overnight. Power structures, mistrust and persisting cultural norms and schemes, as well as institutionalised discrimination, continue to be effective. In post-conflict societies, there are often renewed outbreaks of violence that pose a challenge to sustainable peace.[8]

When social workers support their addressees beyond socially constructed categories and across ethnic-religious boundaries, when they cooperate with others on the basis of their professional code of conduct and universal values, they create spaces that are essential for survival (e.g. social work with women and children of IS supporters, or the children of war rape) and ideally encourage others to do the same. Seifert (2004) speaks of the possibility of silent observation or model-based learning from the socio-structural environment. This could create new impulses and discourses to restore human dignity and to work against hatred. In reference to Zehetbauer (2004), Staub-Bernasconi speaks of the ice breaker or 'hate breaker function' (2004, p. 15).

On the question of how political social work should be, Staub-Bernasconi suggests locating it within the sphere of scientific and professional ethics-based policy. As such, professional social work should take place in crisis areas. This means supporting and strengthening individuals in their needs and at the same time understanding their situation politically. Professional policy begins where it is a matter of making privatised hardships, injustice and debasement public—and

---

[8]In a study by the German Institute for Development Policy (2017), which analysed 28 countries in which a civil war ended after 1990, the researchers come to the conclusion that a) in 50% of the cases there was a relapse into civil war, mostly in the 5 post-war years, b) that post-conflict societies which received more international support were less likely to be affected by the crisis. This applies to all four thematic areas of international peacebuilding, i.e. Socio-Economic Development, Security, Politics, Governance and Social Conflict Transformation, c) that the field of social conflict transformation had a great impact. Both science and politics stress the importance of dealing with the violent past. But according to this study, international donors give the least in this area. (Source: https://www.die-gdi.de/uploads/media/AuS_5.2017.pdf (Access 15. 08. 20).

thus politically debatable—issues (ibid. p. 17). At this level, social work considers the addressees as bearers of individual, political and social rights because they are human beings. By viewing social work as a human rights profession, a start has been made to develop a cosmopolitan reflexivity, where an ethical orientation of its international associations offers another anchor of a *global ethos* of social work (cf. the contribution of *Kristin Sonnenberg* in this volume, which refers to these connections).

The interest of social work in issues of conflict resolution, de-escalation strategies, mediation, peace-keeping (also social peace) and violence prevention has developed rather modestly, and with a view to a systematic discussion (especially in the German-speaking world). It has been underrepresented in theory courses. Yet in recent decades, new areas of social work have developed, which have slowly been reflected in discourse and publications in the German-speaking world. Ruth Seifert's research on the Yugoslavian wars (1991–2001) has produced a first impetus (Seifert 2004a, 2004b). The tightening of the asylum laws (new regulation of Asylum Law in 1993, Asylum Packages 2015 and 2016) has further sharpened the sensitivity towards war traumatisation and towards the necessity of interdisciplinary psychosocial work with refugees, which focuses on the political vulnerability (Ghaderi and van Keuk 2017, p. 258) of its addressees and understands and supports them as acting subjects of their history. In this field in particular, social workers are border workers who balance many ambivalences loaded with tension—otherwise they would perpetuate the refugee regime of isolation, restrictions and fear, and internalize and adopt existing border regimes (ibid. p. 287).

The 2015 European refugee crisis, and the admission of a million people (the majority from Syria, Afghanistan, Iraq) to Germany, has made it clear that war violence which drives people to flee is also a problem of the Global North and poses a continuing challenge for international social work—even if the majority of refugees remain in the Global South. Consequently, the scientific, theoretical and practical dealing with refugees has increased in recent times due to their presence in the Global North (cf. Rehklau 2017; Reklau and Lutz 2018), not least because 'The distant Other [...] has become the inner Other' (Beck 2007, p. 40). According to Seifert (2018), recent interest in discourses on social work in conflict regions is mostly due to the overload of professional and structural deficits that have become evident. In this context of refugee social work, it was even criticised that 'social work does not take seriously its self-image as a human rights profession' (cf. Rehklau 2017, p. 320; Scherr 2015).

The subject of flight and migration is treated from a dual perspective: On the one hand, social work addresses people displaced by war and violence in the receiving countries of the refugees; on the other, it focuses on social work in the post-war and conflict areas in the affected regions. The latter is the focus of the contributions in this volume.

4 Embedding the Topic in Discourses on Knowledge Production

The question of knowledge production, the knowledge canon and the distribution of knowledge is critically reflected within the postcolonial discourse. Key questions are: Who says what? Who should know what?

If international social work is the starting point here, with a view to establishing a human rights perspective (Staub-Bernasconi 2019), it is worth asking how universal these actually are. Are current answers and the knowledge on which they are based globally acceptable?

In fact, internationally comparative social work problematizes and analyzes the construction of the discipline of social work as a Western project that has been exported to other parts of the world (keyword: colonialization of social work). A variety of debates has emerged with regard to the development and relevance of indigenous scientific and professional knowledge in the context of development cooperation. It is well known that regions and countries differ in their definitions of social problems and how to deal with them.

In the Global North, different religious and political readings of social problems and different forms of assistance, fields and goals in social work can be identified. These have evolved from religiously motivated mildness to secularized social-political strategies, encompassing both scientific practice and a tradition of helping.

For the Global South, traditional forms of aid influenced by colonization are postulated, such as solidarity and charity in Islamic countries. In the context of colonization, the import of Northern social work theories and methods is based on the assumption that these would be culture-independent, adaptable in cross-border transfer and universal. Within the history of so-called Northern social work, this assumption manifested itself as English, American and German theories, concepts and methods were interchanged and interwoven during the late 19th and early twentieth centuries. This was due to cooperative work of the pioneers Alice Salomon from Germany, Mary Richmond and Jane Addams from the US Northern parts, and influences from England, where Henrietta and Samuel Barnett had founded the Toynbee Hall in 1884 as part of the settlement movement (cf. Kuhlmann 2013; Braches-Chyrek 2013; Staub-Bernasconi 2018). The second movement comprised re-imports, especially from the US to Germany through the occupying powers, and the return of German scientists after the Second World War in the 1950s and 1960s.

The issues in the South seem to be different and include, amongst others, extreme poverty and population growth, the exclusion of ethnic groups, child soldiers and war (cf. Hecker 2010, p. 49). There are also systematic differences, for example when individual assistance comes up against limits due to cultural and social circumstances. As the potential clientele are not individual people, but families, communities and tribes, the focus on the production of individual relationship work and casework is only partially helpful (Bähr et al. 2016). Of course, this dichotomous confrontation of the Global South and the Global North is itself the subject of debate, as the universality of Western concepts and the homogeneity of the Global South are questioned.

The heterogeneity of the Global South has brought out new trends in social work. In the Latin American context of liberation theology and pedagogy (Paulo Freire), for example, the term *liberation* became relevant, while in Africa and Asia the term *development* has been central to the debates (cf. Rehklau and Lutz 2009). This general debate is summarized under the term 'indigenization' (Lutz and Stauss 2018, p. 266) and implies the further concept of authentication, reconceptualization, radicalization and re-contextualization. 'Indigenization is a product of liberation from the shackles of colonialism and patronage. In the reception of these models, the North must at the same time escape from its own colonial past, liberate itself and become a partner in a dialogue' (Rehklau and Lutz 2009, p. 52).[9]

The aim of all approaches is to develop appropriate knowledge and approaches that are compatible with local conditions and needs. There is no uniformity about what model is relevant at what time and in what place, but the focus is on local framework conditions. These efforts are rich in preconditions and imply that social work must have basic and thorough knowledge of local conditions (Rehklau and Lutz 2009, p. 45).

This requires firstly a profound knowledge of local events politically, psychologically, economically, socially, religiously, and ethnically. Secondly, social workers require knowledge of informal networks, family, kinship, ethnic groups, and communities, as well as problem-solving attempts and coping strategies whose function depends on the existing culture (→ This presupposition-rich local

---

[9]"Indigenisierung ist ein Produkt des Sich Entwindens aus der Klammer des Kolonialismus und der Bevormundung. In der Rezeption dieser Modelle muss der Norden sich zugleich aus seiner eignen Vergangenheit des Kolonialisators entwinden, sich befreien und zum Dialogpartner werden " (vgl. Rehklau and Lutz 2009, p. 52), translated by the authors.

knowledge is at the heart of the contributions of *Karin Mlodoch* and *Berenice Meintjes*).

The range of responses to the different views on what is defined as a problem is an important prerequisite for the understanding and the respective interventions of social work (→ cf. the text by *Rebekka Ehret* in this volume, which explores problem definitions in four regions).

If a volume of supposedly relevant knowledge on the topics of social work in post-war and conflict regions is published here, the question arises in which specific context, in which region and in which historical contexts of the foundation of social work it was developed. This local reality is taken into account in the next section through a short history of social work in the Kurdistan Region in Iraq and a contextualization of the contributions in the context of an international conference.

5 Embedding (International) Social Work in the Kurdistan Region of Iraq

Social work in Kurdistan does not take place in a vacuum. It is contextualized in the structure of society and embedded in cultural traditions, modern transformations and an area affected by permanent injustice, war, violence, experience of suffering and also resistance. The history of social work in Kurdistan as a history of help and of social support practice is certainly older than that of the academic profession.

From an anthropological point of view, differentiated forms of assistance in times of need (relative, neighborly, friendly) develop in everyday culture. A prerequisite is the common cultural construction of a situation defined as an emergency and need for assistance as well as the patterns of support (who, when, how much). Modernization and internationalization have partly changed the traditions of helping in Kurdistan. New social orders, institutions and regulations have re-shaped traditional patterns, but they are not cancelled. From the perspective of post-colonial theory, it is interesting to see how the current phase of the professionalization of social work has come about and what aspects of indigenization play a role.

The history of the teaching of social work in the Kurdistan Region in Iraq is young and goes back to the years 2006/2007. The first Faculty of Social Work was opened at the University of Salahaddin Erbil (USE). The Department of Social Work at the University of Sulaimani (UoS) followed in 2014/2015. This recent history is described by Saleh Karim and Ghaderi (fourthcoming 2021), they identify challenges that seem typical for a pioneering phase. There is, for example, no 'Job Description' defined by the Ministry of Higher Education at present, and so the professional function of social work remains vague, as something of a mix between sociology and psychology. Furthermore, it has not yet established its own professional association, which could represent the interests of social work(ers) in the Kurdistan Region in Iraq and Iraq, initiate important debates in teaching, research and practice, and strengthen regional networking.

As a result of globalization and the opening of the Kurdistan Region to the world from the 1990s onwards,[10] numerous international NGOs and humanitarian organizations came to the region. Their presence created the need for professionally trained social workers. The first Faculty of Social Work at Salahaddin University, which was supported by the Swedish University Dalarna, was influenced by this. A few years later, the Faculty of Social Work at the University of Sulaimani was founded, and a cooperation with the German Protestant University in Bochum was set up during its pioneer phase. In both faculties, the international dialogue on different approaches to social work was groundbreaking, and the graduates were also active in local and international NGOs. In parallel with this, a rich further education and training landscape involving numerous countries provided the social workers and faculty members with insights into various topics of social work from the different perspectives of the respective international experts.

As enriching as international cooperation and the work of NGOs in a conflict region might be, there are obvious gaps between the needs of society and the services provided by international organizations. For example, the international organizations in the Kurdistan Region of Iraq (KR-I) working in the field of social work focus mainly on the provision of psychosocial services, while most

---

[10] Kurdistan-Iraq was cut off from the world until the end of the 1980s and during the reign of Saddam Hussein. The situation changed in the 1990s when, in the wake of the first Gulf War, there was a mass exodus of 1.5 million Kurds to neighboring Turkey and Iran. The images of the survivors from the inhospitable refugee camps in the media startled the public and "international community". The operation "Provide Comfort" of the Gulf War allies began: Based on UN Resolution 688 of April 5, 1991, the Western Allies established a protection and flight ban zone (save haven) in northern Iraq up to the 36th parallel, which was to serve the repatriation of refugees and international security in the region. In the 1990s, numerous local and international organizations came to the Kurdistan Region, in parallel with globalization processes during this period (communication via the Internet, transportation, infrastructure and expansion of airports, etc.). The collapse of the Eastern Bloc and the changes in world politics have led to altered power relations in politics and the economy. The Gulf Wars are not only seen as a fight against the Baathist regime of injustice but also as a war of globalization with the goal of reorganization and for access to resources in the region.

IDPs and refugees more urgently need to meet their basic needs, food and health services. Moreover, the needs of the host communities are given secondary consideration, which may have long-term consequences for social cohesion in the community and society. Undoubtedly the donors play a decisive role in the selection of target groups. However, the question remains whether this gap might not be sufficiently communicated in a partnership dialogue, due to the difference between what is defined as a problem and what is defined as a solution. Another point is the discrepancy in the perception and evaluation of gender issues. Saleh Karim and Ghaderi state that a limited understanding of the Kurdish context, and in particular of gender-based violence and the role legal enforcement, make social work less effective. While many international organizations focus primarily on women and girls, the vulnerable position of men and boys in humanitarian settings tends to be underestimated. This in itself could be described as a form of gender discrimination (ibid).

This analysis coincides with the criticism of feminist postcolonial theorists that gender imaginings were partly disseminated as 'hegemonic gender dichotomies and heteronormativity as a Eurocentric construct only in the course of colonialism, which is why other concepts of gender and sexuality receded into the background' (cf. Hostettler and Vögele 2014, pp. 10). Schirilla also points out that 'gender, some feminist theorists argue, is a Western construct and cannot be transferred in this form to all pre-colonial societies' (Schirilla 2018, p. 4). The problem of gender imaginings is not least a topic in the Orientalism debate and imaginings of local gender relations to create difference and the supposed neediness of Oriental women (cf. the study by Nazand Begikhani (2000) on the images of Kurdish women from the perspective of the debate on Orientalism that goes back to Edward Said). These comments may be sufficient to illustrate that the dialogue is only at the beginning and does not yet answer the question of how colonization or partnership in social work will prevail and in which direction the processes of indigenization (in Kurdistan) will develop.[11]

---

[11] Ghaderi (fourthcoming 2021) discusses the question of whether the use of the term colony and the concept of decolonization of knowledge is appropriate for Kurdistan in light of the historical circumstances.

6 Embedding the Topic as a Reference—Overview of the Contributions in This Book

The approaches to social work in war in and post-conflict regions in this book differ. They point to tensions between local and international, individual and collective perspectives, argue from academic or professional viewpoints, or focus on vulnerable groups.

In the first part, contributions from different theoretical perspectives and positions are represented, contributing knowledge and discussing potentially problematic concepts, which helps to establish fundamental classifications.

Ruth Seifert opened the conference in October 2019 with her keynote speech on the topic of *Social Work, Armed Conflict and Post-War Reconstruction*. Her contribution also opens the volume. She approaches the topic of war and armed conflict from a social-political perspective. This topic, she argues, has not traditionally been central in social work. But the globalization of armed conflicts and the internationalization of social work have made issues of international conflicts and their human consequences a salient topic, confronting social work with new theoretical, political and practical problems. She highlights three of those in her contribution: First, the issue of fundamental changes in social welfare, and—in the wake of it—in social work globally over past decades and their impact on post-conflict social policy and social work. Second, the problems social work and social work education faced in their grassroots work in neoliberal post-conflict reconstruction or *liberal peace*. And third, the need for social work and social work education to confront issues of international politics and the inside of violent conflicts when engaging in post-conflict social work.

In her contribution on *International Social Work and the Global Social Work Statement of Ethical Principles*, *Kristin Sonnenberg* discusses the importance of an international discourse on how social work can address social problems connected to conflicts, crisis and war all over the world at a local and global level. This is interlinked with issues of a shared value base and a shared understanding of the education of professionals. At the international level, three main associations of social work play an important role in shaping a global understanding and possible agreement. In October 2019, already 178 social work associations around the world agreed on the *Global Definition of Social Work* (IFSW and IASSW 2014) and the *Global Social Work Statement of Ethical Principles* (ISFW and IASSW 2018). The assumption is that these agreements and the underlying shared values and standards can strengthen the professional status of social workers at the global and local level. Therefore, different approaches towards social work ethics and possible functions of an ethical code are introduced. Finally, possible implications for international social work, and possible applications of universal principles in different local and cultural circumstances, are discussed.

There are Many Roads to a School of Social Work. Importance of the International for Modern Social Work is the contribution by *Rebekka Ehret*. In her comparative research, she explores the history of four academic schools of social work whose common denominator was, and in some cases still is, the influence of armed conflicts and war. She deals specifically with two histories of the emergence of social work in the Global North (Berkeley, USA and Lucerne, Switzerland) linked to the First World War. She also analyses two cases in the Global South, namely Slemani, Iraq, and Freetown, Sierra Leone. While the first two cases are marked by the national, the others are marked by the international in terms of problem and target group definition, which, according to Ehret, contributes to a post-indigenization paradox. In this sense, the professionalization of social work is seen both as an intervention and as a method of raising public awareness of the social problems of society.

Nausikaa Schirilla reflects upon *Knowledge Production in International Social Work—Postcolonial Perspectives*. Her starting point is the critique of international social work as an export of Western concepts. A key example is the global definition of social work, which has been changed in 2014 and now includes indigenous knowledge as a source of social work. Within her contribution she raises questions about the meaning of indigenous knowledge societies where there is no tradition of social work, ways of adapting social work to specific local and cultural contexts and the barriers in current thinking that prevent us from answering these questions. Her statements and her analysis are based on postcolonial conceptions and their critique. Finally, she discusses consequences for the international community.

Based on her longstanding years of research and work experience, *Karin Mlodoch* reflects in her article entitled *Systematising Local Knowledge: Hierarchies, Power Relations and Decontextualisation in West–East Knowledge Transfer* on the psycho-social counselling work with female survivors of violence in the Iraqi region of Kurdistan. It notes the current influence of mostly Western concepts of trauma, psychosocial and social work in the region and takes this as an opportunity to take a critical look at the hierarchies and colonial aspects inherent in West–East knowledge transfer and its tendencies to decontextualize and marginalize local knowledge and practices. Referring to examples of local practice in processing trauma and psychosocial work, she presents approaches to the systematization of local practices and knowledge of social work and takes a critical position on the construction of a dichotomy between local and global knowledge and on the risk of 'culturalization' of different approaches to social work. She advocates a revitalized debate on the development of participatory and equal platforms and mechanisms for knowledge transfer, theory–practice transfer and knowledge exchange in the field of international (psycho)social work.

Her argumentation is supported by *Berencie Meintjes* in her contribution *Community-Based Psychosocial Work to Change the Cycle of Violence in Post Conflict Areas*. With regard to South Africa and Kurdistan, the method of community-based interventions is introduced. Working with examples of concrete projects from her many years of experience as a psychologist and counsellor, Meintjes poses provocative questions about the model of justice that is used to promote reconciliation and participatory community development. South Africa is still one of the most unequal societies in the world, even after official processes aimed at restorative justice. Berenice Meintjes' research shows that a holistic approach to support is needed as an emerging model of social work in conflict areas, which includes economic strengthening such as income-generating activities and education in combination with psycho-social support. An example from the Ubuntu community shows how a traditional and religious cleansing ritual contributed to reconciliation processes. One of the main questions Berenice Meintjes discusses are: How can we collectively and meaningfully intervene to disrupt the cycle of violence, which often takes place in post-conflict areas? Violence, displacement, loss of resources and the breakdown of the social fabric of family and community life often lead to ongoing cycles of violence, including revenge, displaced aggression such as domestic violence and sexual assault, early marriages, crime, corruption and extremism. The contribution shows the importance of working with survivor support groups to address their needs, and with solidarity movements to prevent conflict, abuse, inequality and division. All these form a part of empowering and participative processes.

In the second part of this book, the focus is on vulnerabilities caused by armed conflicts and warfare, since the regular consequences of war include sexualized violence and flight movement. These contributions provide an example of two themes to highlight the fact that wars produce vulnerable groups whose bodies are degraded, injured, and killed: children, women, and refugees as displaced people.

Cinur Ghaderi's contribution *Children born of Wartime Rapes—An Analysis from a Gender-Sensitive and Psychosocial Perspective* deals with the consequences of mass rape and sexual violence, which are still part of war strategies, with a focus on the Yazidi women in the ISIS war. These mothers and their children born from such brutal attacks experience psychosocial burdens such as social exclusion and stigmatization. Finally, the existence of these children raises human rights and ethical-normative questions about the orientation points for society and law.

Should they focus on origin and paternal line, or the perspective of human rights and children? This paper reconstructs the gender specific dynamics of armed conflict and political violence. Taking into account the historical, individual and social conditions, a framework is designed to understand the specific problems and multiple loads of victimized mothers and their children born of rape in the field of psychosocial sciences. In particular, to bring up a painful subject, these forms of violence should not be reduced to a rupture or break in civilisation, but must be perceived as a continuity of violence in society. For only normative gender orders that already exist prepare the ground for the legitimation of sexualized violence in the context of war and are to be read in this sense as a continuity of existing conditions.

In their article *The Refugee as a Stigmatized Individual—Spoiled Identities, Possible Causes and Courses of Action for Social Work*, Lisa-Marie Dünnebacke and *Kristin Goetze* explore the mechanisms of exclusion to which refugees from war regions are subject by means of legal restrictions. Using Goffman's stigma theory as a starting point, they raise the question to which extent flight is understood as a stigma. According to the authors, the special value of stigma theory lies in the fact that it allows a look at the consequences of exclusion for the self-image of refugees and their everyday survival strategies, but without falling back on individualizing interpretations of a socially conditioned problematic situation. Instead, it allows for an understanding of the constitutive conditions of exclusion. They evaluate this analytical perspective as more purposeful than monological ways of thinking, and more appropriately linked to concepts of transcultural competence and social justice.

Of course, these contributions are not exhaustive, but rather initiate the realization of a globalized world and its implications for theory and practice of social work. They cannot claim to present a truly diverse and inclusive perspective. It is striking that the authors are all women, and mostly white women. Certainly, this stimulates thinking from a post-colonial perspective. Can these women be considered allies?[12] What excluding factors contributed to this selection? Language, place of origin, networks? Coincidence and pragmatism? In fact, from day one,

---

[12] Allies is a term inspired by Hanna Arendt's philosophy and has found its way into the social justice and diveristy and racism-critical debate. "Being allied describes, in the style of Arendt, a kind of political friendship in which the concerns of others are the concerns of others—without being paternalistic. It is a specific form of solidarity, in which not the ego is at the center, but the others who are not like you. (Czollek et al. 2019, p. 40). In other words, a conception of action in which "the common interest of the world is not based on an identitary affiliation to a particular group, but rather on the common interest of the world" (ibid, p. 210). It is not about one's own sensitivities, not about the affirmation of the other for

we have been thinking about these issues and ways of dealing with them. At present, we see this as a strength with respect to the idea of a special focus on the topic of war. There are still points of criticism, there is still a process, but it is certain that the international dialogue will be continued with the will to establish equal partnerships.

We hope that our book and the individual contributions invite readers to widen their understanding of new contexts and ideas for social work in regions of postwar and post-conflict areas, to reflect upon the role of social workers in international fields of work and to critically think about different starting points, whether they lie in geographical origins or in political and ethical attitudes.

References

Bähr, C., Homfeldt, H. G., Schröder, C., & Schweppe, C. (Eds.). (2014). *Weltatlas Soziale Arbeit. Jenseits aller Vermessungen* (pp. 9–32). Beltz Juventa: Weinheim und Basel.
Beck, U. (2007). *Weltrisikogesellschaft. Auf der Suche nach der verlorenen Sicherheit.* Frankfurt/Main: Suhrkamp Verlag .
BICC, Bonn International Center for Conversion/Bundeszentrale für Politische Bildung. (2011). Kriegsdefinitionen und Kriegstypologien. https://sicherheitspolitik.bpb.de/m1/articles/definitions-of-war-and-conflict-typologies. Accessed: 27. Aug. 2020.
BMVG, Bundesministerium für Verteidigung. (2016). Humanitäres Völkerrecht in bewaffneten Konflikten. https://www.bmvg.de/resource/blob/93612/f16edcd7b796ff3b43b239039cfcc8d1/b-02-02-10-download-handbuch-humanitaeres-voelkerrecht-in-bewaffneten-konflikten-data.pdf. Accessed: 25. Aug. 2020.
Braches-Chyrek, R. (2013). *Jane Addams, Mary Richmond und Alice Salomon.* Opladen: Verlag Barbara Budrich.
Bundeszentrale für Politische Bildung. Sicherheitspolitik. https://sicherheitspolitik.bpb.de/m1/glossary. Accessed: 29. Sept. 2018.
Czollek, L. C., Perko, G., & Weinbach, H. (2019). *Praxishandbuch Social Justice und Diversity* (2nd ed.). Beltz Juventa: Weinheim.
Dülffer, J. (2016). Alte und neue Kriege. Gewaltkonflikte und Völkerrecht seit dem 19. Jahrhundert. In: Aus Politik und Zeitgeschichte/bpb.de, https://www.bpb.de/apuz/232960/alte-und-neue-kriege. Accessed: 26. Aug. 2020.
Duman, N., & Snoubar, Y. (2016). Importance of school social work in war and conflicts zone. *European Journal of Social Science Education and Research, 3*(2), 191–194. https://doi.org/10.26417/ejser.v6i2.pp.191-194.
Engelke, E., Borrmann, S., & Spatschek, C. (2009). *Theorien der Sozialen Arbeit Eine Einführung* (5. überarbeitete und erweiterte ed.). Freiburg im Breisgau: Lambertus-Verlag.

---

the construction of aptitude, but rather "topic- and action-related reflection of structures of discrimination" (ibid).

Hecker, S. (2010). *Soziale Arbeit in der Entwicklungszusammenarbeit. Bedeutung, Herausforderung und Verantwortung systemisch-konstruktivistischer Hilfe.* Oldenburg: Paul Freire. https://onlinelibrary.wiley.com/doi/full/https://doi.org/10.1111/ijsw.12417.

HIIK, Heidelberg Institute for International Conflict Research. Methodology. https://hiik.de/. Accessed: 27. Aug. 2020.

HIIK. (2020). Heidelberg Institute for International Conflict Research. Conflict Barometer. https://hiik.de/konfliktbarometer/aktuelle-ausgabe/. Accessed: 27. Aug. 2020.

Kuhlmann, C. (2013). *Geschichte Sozialer Arbeit I. Studienbuch* (3rd ed.). Wochenschau-Verl: Schwalbach/Ts.

McMahon, P. C. (2019). *Das NGO-Spiel. Zur ambivalenten Rolle von Hilfsorganisationen in Postkonfliktländern.* Hamburg: Verlag des Hamburger Instituts für Sozialforschung.

Nazand, B. (2000). Das Bild der kurdischen Frau in der orientalischen Literatur des neunzehnten Jahrhunderts. In S. Hajo, C. Borck, & E. Savelsberg (Eds.), *Kurdische Frauen und das Bild der kurdischen Frau* (pp. 51–77). Münster: LIT Verlag.

Rehklau, C. (2017). Flüchtlinge als Adressat_innen Sozialer Arbeit? Sozialarbeiterwissenschaftlicher Zugang. In C. Ghaderi & T. Eppenstein (Eds.), *Flüchtlinge – Multiperspektivische Zugänge* (pp. 305–323). Wiesbaden: VS Verlag.

Rehklau, C., & Lutz, R. (2009). Partnerschaft oder Kolonisation? Thesen zum Verhältnis des Nordens zur Sozialarbeit des Südens. In: Wagner L., Lutz R. (eds) *Internationale Perspektiven Sozialer Arbeit* (pp. 31–53). VS Verlag für Sozialwissenschaften. Weinheim.

Rehklau, C., & Lutz, R. (2018). Migration und Flucht. In L. Wagner, R. Lutz, C. Rehklau, & F. Ross (Eds.), *Handbuch Internationale Soziale Arbeit. Dimensionen - Konflikte - Positionen* (pp. 240–255). Weinheim: Springer.

Saleh Karim, L., & Ghaderi, C. (2021). *Teaching social work in Kurdistan region of Iraq.* Wiesband: Springer VS.

Scherr, A. (2015). Soziale Arbeit Mit Flüchtlingen. *Sozial Extra, 4,* 16–19.

Schirilla, N. (2018). Diversität in einer postkolonialen Perspektive. In Pfaller-Rott, M. E. Gómez-Hernández, & H. Soundari (Eds.), *Soziale Vielfalt* (pp. 3–12). Wiesbaden: Springer VS.

Schwank, N. (2019). Konzepte und Methoden zur Erfassung von Kriegen und politisch motivierter Gewalt. bpb. https://www.bpb.de/internationales/weltweit/innerstaatliche-konflikte/294092/konzepte-und-methoden. Accessed: 27. Aug. 2020.

Seifert, R. (2018). Armed Conflict and Social Work. In L. Wagner, R. Lutz, C. Rehklau, & F. Ross (Eds.), *Internationale Perspektiven Sozialer Arbeit. Dimensionen – Themen – Organisationen* (2nd ed., pp. 181–193). Weinheim: Beltz Juventa.

Seifert, R. (Ed.). (2004a). *Soziale Arbeit und kriegerische Konflikte.* Münster: LIT.

Seifert, R. (Ed.). (2004b). *Gender, Identität und kriegerischer Konflikt. Das Beispiel des ehemaligen Jugoslawien.* Münster: Lit.

Sen, A. (2007). *Die Identitätsfalle. Warum es keinen Krieg der Kulturen gibt.* München: Beck-Verlag.

Staub-Bernasconi, S. (2004). Kriegerische Konflikte und Soziale Arbeit. Ein altes und neues Thema der Sozialarbeit. In R. Seifert (Ed.), *Soziale Arbeit und kriegerische Konflikte* (pp. 9–19). Münster: LIT.

Staub-Bernasconi, S. (2018). *Die Soziale Arbeit als Handlungswissenschaft.* Opladen: Verlag Barbara Budrich.

Staub-Bernasconi, S. (2019). *Menschenwürde, Menschenrechte, Soziale Arbeit. Die Menschenrechte vom Kopf auf die Füße stellen.* Opladen: Verlag Barbara Budrich.

Zehetbauer, L. (2004). Social work and substainable peace: The role of social work in postwar reconstruction. In R. Seifert (Ed.), *Soziale Arbeit und kriegerische Konflikte* (pp. 71–94). LIT: Münster.

Social Work, Armed Conflict and Post-War Reconstruction

Ruth Seifert

Abstract

War and armed conflict have not traditionally been central topics in social work. The globalisation of armed conflicts and the internationalisation of social work have made issues of international conflicts and their human consequences a salient topic confronting social work with new theoretical, political and practical problems. Three of those will be highlighted:

1. The issue of fundamental changes in social welfare, and—in the wake of it—in social work globally over past decades and their impact on post-conflict social policy and social work.
2. The problems social work and social work education faced in their grassroots work in neoliberal post-conflict reconstruction or *liberal peace*.
3. The need for social work and social work education to confront issues of international politics and the inside of violent conflicts when engaging in post-conflict social work.

Keywords

Social work · Post-war reconstruction · Armed conflict

R. Seifert (✉)
Department of Applied Social and Health Sciences, University of Applied Sciences Regensburg, Regensburg, Germany
E-Mail: ruth-seifert@t-online.de

1   War and Armed Conflicts

War and armed conflict have not been classical topics in social work discourse. Even though those who are commonly called the founders of social work—such as Alice Salomon and Jane Addams—were aware of the social significance of armed conflict and adopted a pacifist stance (cf. Schüler 2004, p. 184), what political crises, war and armed conflict actually mean for social work theory and practice has not been pursued systematically. Only recently has interest been drawn to the fact that social work is happening in crisis areas and, nolens volens, has to react to political crises abroad and at home, and that this 'social work in extremis' (Lavalette and Iokamidis 2011) is underresearched and undertheorized. The often decried localized focus of social work in almost all countries has contributed to this blind spot. Social work discourse has largely stayed within the confines of a national or, at best, a European/North American perspective and has not sufficiently kept pace with the globalisation of social problems including the effects (and the causes) of armed conflicts and their world-wide repercussions (cf. Lavalette and Iokamidis 2011; Strauss and Lutz 2016). However, in view of international developments over the past decades, 'the discipline can no longer function effectively without an understanding of the global environment' (Yesufu 2009, p. 80). In particular, international crises and armed conflict have become a social work issue because of the effects they produce, which, in times of globalization, have become social policy concerns in most countries and as such are fed into social work practice. To take Germany as an example, after 2015 and in the wake of the so-called 'refugee crisis', refugee work has become a centerpiece of social work practice (cf. Filsinger 2017). This confrontation of social work with the spillover effects of armed conflict has made the blind spots of social work practice obvious. While, by all accounts, social workers in Germany were not performing too badly given the scarcity of resources, the social work sector was not sufficiently prepared for the refugee situation in the wake of 2015, neither regarding theoretical or political background knowledge, nor organisational issues or the practical handling of the situation. Even though matters of 'interculturalism' have entered social work education some time ago, and even though various authors have called for an involvement of social work in peacebuilding and conflict resolution for some time (cf. Kafula 2016, pp. 115; Lavalette/ Ioakimidis 2011; Yesufu 2009), issues of armed conflicts and their impact on a possible clientele are only slowly becoming a major topic in social work discourse.

Globalization and the globalized effects of so-called *'new wars'* have brought social work in the more developed countries into even more immediate contact with armed conflict and political crises in regions of the Global South. The phenomenon of so-called 'new wars' is relevant for social work. The 'new war'-concept describes assumed changes in the nature of warfare, with an increased participation of non-state actors such as militia warlords, mercenaries, paramilitaries and criminal gangs unleashing new levels of brutal violence primarily aimed not at the military enemy, but at civilians (cf. Münkler 2002). Evidence of this development is the steadily increasing number of civilian casualties. While in the wars of the first half of the twentieth century about 90% of the casualties were combatants, this number is reversed for wars of the late twentieth century with about 80% of casualties being civilians (cf. ibid., p. 28). Civilians in new wars are exposed to extreme—and possibly increasing—acts of violence and atrocities, including human rights violations that have led to new definitions of what we mean by 'security' and to new political agendas. Among the phenomena discussed is gender-specific violence against females, but, as more recent evidence reveals, also against males (e.g. Couturier 2012; Dolan 2014; Zipfel et al. 2019). Systematic attacks on civilians have created 'durable disorders', producing protracted conflicts and pitching people 'into states of violent turmoil, confused movement, precarious existence and deep grief' (Turshen 2019, p. 74)—situations which produce new challenges for humanitarian help. The globalized nature of present-day conflicts has increased flight movements which carry the fallout of new wars into the Global North. Moreover, as social work increasingly extends beyond the borders of the nation state, the profession is increasingly forced to deal with post-war issues that result from the protracted conflicts of our time.

'New wars' is a contested concept, and it has been debated whether what has been described as 'new wars' is really a new phenomenon or has only gained greater publicity recently due to greater awareness and rejection of the use of violence in many parts of the world. As far as social work practice is concerned, this question is of minor importance: Whether new or not, in times of globalization the consequences of these conflicts are globalized; whether new or not, the plight and suffering of the civilian population has gained greater visibility and attention. Refugee flows are reaching the Northern hemisphere, thus impacting directly on social work practice inside, and increasingly also outside, the immediate conflict zones.

As 'local' social work is confronted with questions that reach beyond localized boundaries, it is also confronted with fields of knowledge which so far have not been part of the social work discourse. Just as dealing with 'poverty' in practical work requires knowledge of the causes and backgrounds of social inequality, if social workers are to do more than just engage in social engineering, the effects of armed conflicts cannot be separated from their causes and backgrounds. In the same vein, social work will have to deal with issues of post-conflict reconstruction, peacebuilding and reconciliation. In the following, an attempt will be made to cast light on selected issues dealing with the interrelation between armed conflict, peacebuilding and social work.

2   Social Work, Post-Conflict Reconstruction and 'Liberal Peace'

Post-war reconstruction is closely tied to the concept of *'liberal peace'*. In academic and political discourse on post-war reconstruction, the catchword 'liberal peace' serves as shorthand for the process of establishing a very specific kind of 'peace' in post-war reconstruction over the past few decades. While the 'liberal peace project' has come under quite some scrutiny, and while the actual practice of 'liberal peace' may show inconsistencies, face pitfalls and meet with local forms of resistance which change the realities and success stories of the project (cf. Selby 2013), there is nevertheless consensus that post-conflict reconstruction has been geared towards a defined project of liberalisation which is still well and alive framing post-war reconstruction efforts: (Neo-)liberal peace pursues state-building in post-conflict settings (which are almost exlusively in the Global South) modelled along the lines of a 'neoliberal economy', a 'neoliberal society' and 'neoliberal personalities'. These are political and economic agendas that are also rampant in the Northern Hemisphere (cf. Duffield 2001; Richmond 2009). 'Liberal peace' or 'neoliberal peace' describes practices that are put forward by the so-called international community placing 'state-building' in post-conflict settings on top of its agenda—an approach generally described as a 'governance approach' to peacebuilding. State-building is to guarantee 'that neoliberal political economies can be institutionalized' (Pugh 2011, p. 3). This state-building effort aims at establishing formal democracy and liberate the markets, thus insinuating that 'Western liberalism represents the ultimate evolutionary direction for all societies' (ibid.). As a result, practical projects –in academia as well as in the field of social provisions or social work—nolens volens have to work within the frameworks that seek to establish 'liberal peace'. Duffield goes as far as to contend that NGOs, which are the main implementing institutions of social work in post-conflict regions, contrary to their self-understanding as apolitical, humanitarian helpers, are hidden agents of a (neo-) liberal agenda. While aid workers see themselves as helpers and advisers, as someone standing outside the system, in reality, so Duffield, they are an integral part of the liberal peace project influencing behaviour by enforcing concepts such as 'self-reliance', 'personal autonomy', 'self-responsibility' and supporting the 'entrepreneurial self' by facilitating economic development through micro-credits and specific educational efforts aimed at promoting a free-market economy (cf. Duffield 2007, pp. 32; cf. also Taylor 2010, pp. 154).

The neoliberal agenda is not only pursued in post-conflict reconstruction. Indeed, it has been posing a problem for social work and social work education in the Global North for quite some time. Some authors even talk about 'North going South' (Duffield 2019, p. 121), assuming that in the long run, the North may catch up with the South—'catch-up, that is, in terms of the global future of work, at least for the majority being a precarious and resilience-demanding existence under conditions of permanent economic emergency' (Streeck 2011, pp. 5). Until several decades ago, social work in the Global North has been linked with the development of welfare states and could not be separated from the political agendas that have informed welfare state developments. The neoliberal deconstruction of welfare states in the wake of the neoliberal reconstruction of the economy and of society in the Global North has resulted in a downsizing of welfare provisions as well as a commodification of social services. The commodification of services in turn has turned many social workers into 'service providers' who sell a service under market conditions or semi-market conditions. The neo-social transformation of the welfare state in the social work arena is, among others, to be achieved by turning social work into a business -like profession (the introduction of 'new public management' as *the* management model to be pursued in public services, including social work, has been a case in point). The economisation and managerialization of social work aims to create a 'social market' that works on the basis of economic efficiency and cost-effectiveness, promising cheaper and better service provision as well as more influence of service users and more professional efficiency. A Dutch study confirms what has been predicted on the basis of theoretical analyses, and what social workers on the ground have experienced for a long time: Modelling welfare organisations according to business standards and treating social services as 'products' while calling clients 'customers' does not recognize the specific working conditions of social work. Indeed, it makes social work less effective and undermines the professionalism and the quality of the discipline. It strengthens neither service users nor social workers, but, as many studies as well as practitioners' observations have shown, it deprofessionalizes social work and deteriorates working conditions while strengthening the economic interests of service providing organisations and financiers (cf. Tonkens 2019; Marthinsen et al., 2019; Kessl 2013). In consequence, the main theoretical and political trajectory in the social work literature over the past decades has been the possible resistance social work can mobilize against the neoliberal transformation of society, the deconstruction of the welfare state and in its wake the deprofessionalization of social work (e.g. Spolander et al., 2014; Marthinsen et al., 2019).

But what does the onslaught of neoliberal agendas mean when social work is taking place in post-conflict regions? It means that what has been happening in the Global North is replicated in the Global South—often under aggravated circumstances. The neoliberal terms in the post-war context are primarily set by international institutions such as the World Bank and the International Monetary Fund—two institutions whose objectives are to bring together the world markets and ensure that economic and social conditions are conducive to capitalist reproduction. The centerpieces of this policy are market liberalisation, privatization and structural reforms that dismantle the welfare state, coupled with an emphasis on human rights and the rule of law. These policies are often cloaked in a way that makes them appear as being informed by either 'disinterested benevolence', or they are presented as 'the natural outcome of abstract forces too powerful for humanity to resist' (Taylor 2010, p. 158). However, liberal peace is not an act of God: It is top-down, elite-led and rests on official processes (cf. Richmond 2010, p. 22).

What is interesting for social work is the fact that the World Bank as well as the International Monetary Fund pursues a specific model of social protection in post-conflict regions that is not in accord with the idea of the welfare state that had developed in the wake of industrialisation in Europe. The traditional welfare states which came into existence in the Global North (particularly continental Europe) in the late 19th and first half of the twentieth century, had an idea of social protection as a human right, requiring inclusive schemes for the bulk of the population. They were often based on an insurance system that provided the members of the system with legal rights to social provisions, particularly health insurance and old age care including pensions. On the other hand, there is a conception of social protection as a special and exceptional service aimed at the poor and the needy exclusively, while social security for the rest of society has to be taken care of individually and not, as the traditional welfare state would have it, be organized within a system of solidarity and mutual responsibility. In the second model, social support is handed out under certain conditions and dependent on recipients fulfilling certain demands. While the first model works on the basis of contributions of all members into an insurance system and state responsibility for organising this system, the second puts personal responsibility and private provisions at its center, works with a low level of state investment, prefers low-cost programmes and supports austerity measures that liberalize the economy from what is considered too heavy a load of social payments. The main actors in post-war reconstruction, the World Bank and the International Monetary Fund, clearly pursue the second model and discourage the first (cf. Kidd 2018). This is problematic—if not disastrous—for post-conflict societies and communities that have gone through a system breakdown and are not in a position to provide sufficient welfare or employment to generate a market-oriented transformation that would give a boost to the economy (cf. Pugh 2010, p. 268). As has been described for almost all post-war regions that have been exposed to this policy, the outcome of this kind of 'liberalisation' of the economy and of the social realm is the production of a 'surplus population', i.e. people without work, without regular income, without access to education or social provisions. Liberal peace, according to Duffield, 'rather than being concerned with reducing the economic gap between rich and poor countries, or extending to the latter the levels of social protection existing in the former' (Duffield 2006 p. ix), attempts to manage the destabilizing social effects of this situation by establishing a technology of security and by adapting individuals to unstable and 'uninsured' circumstances. These uninsured circumstances have given rise to a 'survival economy', i.e. an economy without social security for the majority, that requires these 'uninsured populations' to struggle through on remittances, foreign aid, barter, an informal economy and undeclared earnings (cf. Duffield 2001, pp. 30). For liberal peace in post-conflict areas, institutionalized welfare and social security (which, it should be remembered, are central concerns in social work) are anathema to the economic agenda (cf. Pugh 2010, p. 268). This is mirrored by the fact that international financial assistance, which post-conflict regions generally are vitally dependent on, is predicated on macro-economic conditions that prescribe a reduced role for the state and a minimum of social policy in favour of individual entrepreneurship and initiative, of privatisation and business incentives—also in the social sector. In the Global South, we are dealing with a policy of 'carrots and sticks where cooperation paves the way for development assistance and access to the wider networks of global governance, while non-cooperation risks varying degrees of conditionality and isolation' (Duffield 2001, p. 34). As in the Global North, the ultimate aim is that people are no longer instructed to act according to the expectations of a liberalised market-economy, but to do it willingly themselves—in other words: to gear human subjectivities to the needs of the liberalized markets. It follows that neoliberalism is not only an economic project, but one involving society as a whole—including the very make-up of our being, our subjectivities. These transformations have been taking place in the Global North and are enforced in the Global South.

3 Liberal Peace, Social Work and the Transformation of Subjectivities

Liberal peace (as the neoliberal project in general) is not only about economic and social policies or state structures and institutions. It is essentially also about a reconstruction of subjectivity that fits the neoliberal model. In the Global North, the enforcement of this kind of subjectivity is well advanced, even though not yet hegemonic. Social work is located at the juncture between the individual and society. As a result, social work is by its very nature always involved in the development of personalities and the shaping of subjectivities. The entanglement of social work in the production of neoliberal mentalities and conducts of life, and the constitution of subjectivity in the Global North have been amply described in the social work literature (e.g. Webb 2000; Kessl and Otto 2012; Kessl 2013; Chassé 2014). In post-war regions, the production of neoliberal subjectivities is also part of the programme, and humanitarian aid and post-conflict social work also play a role—particularly as an unprecedented level of humanitarian aid has developed over the past decades (Maglajlic 2011, pp. 105).

Here, we find additional pitfalls which psychosocial helpers face. While social work is always involved in subjectivity formation, the question is whether this is done with an awareness of one's activities, and on the basis of social work values as put down by the leading social work organisations—such as the International Federation of Social Workers and the International Association of Schools of Social Work –, or unconsciously and as part of an agenda that has been determined elsewhere, and by agencies that are ultimately antagonistic towards social work values. Under conditions of liberal peace, social work initiatives must function within INGO and NGO systems that work within the overall framework set by the relevant economic organisations. In this vein, practices in post-conflict regions have come under scrutiny, which, while appearing 'apolitical' or politically innocuous, have come to be seen as associated with the neoliberal project. These are practices of psychosocial support and a specific kind of help to self-help—in other words the classical social work activities.

The role which apolitical and unreflected social work can play has been exposed in Pupavac's scathing criticism of psychosocial intervention in post-conflict areas (cf. Pupavac 2001, 2002; also Mlodoch 2017). Psychosocial intervention in conflict areas, Pupavac claims, has been obsessed with the *psychological and emotional* state of survivors and refugees. 'Traumatization' has been the central catchword to grasp the situation of those affected. While whole populations may be without proper housing, sanitary facilities, food and medical provisions, separated from their families, without secure legal status and without perspectives for the future, 'trauma counseling', 'education programmes', 'therapeutic intervention' and similar offers have been a standard response from psychosocial helpers. On the other hand, social workers have reported that psychological disturbances that had been treated over prolonged periods of time disappeared within weeks once clients were provided with a safe status, safe housing and family reunion. In the same vein, Semigina and Gusak point out that the most pressing issues social workers identified in refugees in the Ukrainian war zone were not of a psychological nature, but had to do with provisions of food, housing, and information about the whereabouts of family members (cf. Semigina and Gusak 2015).

Thus, by placing certain problems and methods at the forefront that emphasize the individual, psychological and de-politicized problems of survivors, psychosocial help becomes complicit with the objectives of neoliberal peace. The argument runs like this: If the living conditions are not conducive to individual or collective well-being, it is not the conditions that are to be changed. Instead, the individual and the collectivity have to adapt to ruling circumstances and become flexible, resilient and accepting of whatever conditions they encounter. The often used PTSD model may—inadvertently—be a support in shaping the wanted neoliberal subjectivities. Despite considerable criticism regarding its validity, the traumatisation of populations is still frequently assessed with the PTSD model, which is also used widely in social work (cf. Mlodoch 2017, pp. 32). Within this model, the social and political problems people are suffering from are individualized, psychologised and pathologized. While the validity of these practices is not contested for individual cases, they seem misplaced when they are applied to whole populations whose needs could be better met by working towards the establishment of a social system that would guarantee social and economic security and provide perspectives for a future life. However, 'therapeutic governance' and pedagogical measures make sense in the context of 'neoliberal peace'. Neoliberal peace is arguably not aiming at an economy that would provide secure working conditions and social safety. Instead, the supposedly nascent economy in conflict areas is to be based on a maximum of competition within the labour force and strict privatization of all services including social services. Thus, it is not economic and social conditions that are to be rebuilt in such a way as to serve the 'traumatized' population; instead, subjectivity is pathologized and colonized in order to meet the demands of the intervening powers. This is done by psychologizing humanitarian aid and offering individual psychological treatment for problems that are clearly collective and have political and social causes (cf. Pupavac 2001, 2002; also Beristain, pp. 143).

In other words: Subjectivies are to be made resilient, flexible and accepting of the newly introduced conditions. Unreflective and well-meaning helpers may thus be complicit in a modernized colonialization effort that works with Western psychosocial concepts and individualizing methods. These methods are not so much suited to improving the conditions of those concerned, but all the more suited to establishing new socio-economic conditions and subjectivities in accord with the exigencies of a neoliberal peace model. This includes the individualization of subjectivities and glossing over indigenous coping methods.[1]

In a similar vein, Schellhaas and Seegers state that aid work which claims to be apolitical, and focuses on the micro-level, engages in unreflective practice and is thereby complicit in legitimising the dominant ideology. This ideology, however, is not about the interests of local populations but about global economic interests, and obscures the fact that aid work spreads the values and priorities of a transnational class in association with local elites that profit from the neoliberal transformation of society (cf. Schellhaas and Seegers 2009, p. 10). More often than not, these are not the values of academically and ethically based social work. This 'therapeutic governance' of war-affected populations and persons focuses the individual in trying to mobilize capacities for coping with a situation that would basically require establishing a social (and for that matter economic) system which could guarantee the fulfilment of basic needs, provide safety and perspectives for a future life. In neoliberal peace, on the other hand, the micromanagement of people's lives gains increasing importance. Social work engaging in 'micromanagement' is therefore in particular danger of joining in the psychologizing and individualization of social problems. Nolens volens, social work is politically positioned.

4   The Political Side of Trauma

Psychosocial support has yet another side which poses problems that are not obvious at first sight. Psychosocial support and psychological therapy are generally understood to be apolitical. Becker has pointed out that by trying to keep

---

[1] An example is Nita Luci's description of the handling of war rapes by psychosocial (feminist) organisations in Kosovo/a. It is a commonplace that, as distinct from Bosniak women, Kosovar women did not talk about their war experiences, even though there is evidence that mass rapes took place in the country in 1999. Psychosocial organisations from the Global North had no doubt how this was to be explained: Due to patriarchal suppression, the women did not dare to talk, thus depriving themselves of the necessary psychosocial help. Luci points out that the situation might have been more complex. In a country with a "culture of silence ", as which Kosovohas been described, to remain silent may have been a local coping mechanism – if not for all, at least for an undefined number of women. Moreover, being silent may also have been an act of resistance.

politics out of the psychosocial process when we are dealing with survivors of political and violent conflict, social and individual processes are split up in what he calls 'a reactionary manner' (cf. Becker 2014, p. 40). This 'reactionary manner' may not be coincidental: Mlodoch (cf. 2017, pp. 42) has pointed out the theoretical closeness of neoliberal thought and an apolitical and decontextualized trauma concept and thus the production of neoliberal subjectivies by psychological means: Reducing trauma treatment to 'methods' that are detached from the material and political context in which the trauma was inflicted facilitates the depolitization of social and political problems, the homogenisation and pathologizing of individuals and last but not least the marketization of trauma treatment (cf. also Adams et al. 2019).

If psychosocial work does not acknowledge that clients have been victimized as a result of political processes and instead concentrates exclusively on the individual's psychological state, it denies that *political* events and *political* actors have caused this suffering. Extreme suffering is never merely a destruction of the individual, nor merely a consequence of socio-political events, *it is always both.* What happens in circumstances of political violence is the transformation of a social process into individual suffering and illness (cf. Becker, ibid., pp. 59). Social and political processes are very different in nature, and the individual 's political and cultural position in these processes varies depending on the particular political and cultural context. Severe suffering and what is called 'trauma' can therefore not be grasped sufficiently by measuring it with a one-size-fits-all template such as the inflationary (and amply critisised) use of the PTSD concept which completely glosses over the (political) context into which suffering is embedded and makes it a problem of the individual person—an 'individual illness'. Becker convincingly argues that psychosocial help has to make an effort to deal with the social, political and cultural context and to recognize that was has been done to the suffering person has been done for a reason and has been part of strategies and policies. Our understanding of suffering must remain insufficient and superficial if we assume that the Syrians, Iraqis, Eritreans, Pakistanis and people with war experiences in other contexts, men, women and LGBTI, all share the same kind of 'trauma', use similar coping mechanisms and are open to the same methods of intervention, which have been detected and distributed in advance in handy one-size-fits-all 'best practice' manuals.[2] Research on politically caused trauma has

---

[2]In a similiar vein, Pupavac asked why one should assume that after the war in 1999, Kosovo-Albanians who had taken a step towards the independence of the country and could, to some extent, be considered "victorious – and were the main targets of psychosocial post-war programs – would respond to war in the same way as the models of the PTSD-model, viz.,

shown that psychosocial help and therapy remain ineffective without an understanding of the political character of the inflicted trauma and requires the helpers to take a political and moral stance. Thus, Martin-Baró showed how politically caused traumata become chronic if political circumstances do not change and the political context of atrocities is not addressed (cf. Merk 2001, p. 17). For social work, this means that an understanding of international politics and armed conflict have to enter social work education to a much larger extent than has been the case up until now. It does not suffice to indulge in 'trauma work' or whatever description is used. 'Trauma' has to be understood as a psychological *and* a political phenomenon. In order to be able 'to help the person', empathy and psychological methods are not enough.

Finally, it has been noted in various scenarios that victims and survivors of political violence and torture need to understand what has happened to them and for what reasons it has been inflicted on them if they are to have a chance of entering into a coping process. Bettelheim emphasised that concentration camp inmates coped more successfully if they had an explanation for what happened to them (cf. Bettelheim 1990). In the same vein, psychosocial helpers in the wake of the mass rapes in former Yugoslavia reported that the healing process in surviving women made a qualitative leap if they understood that they had been attacked as symbolic representatives of their ethnic or national group, and that the purpose of the sexual victimisation was to destroy the social fabric of their respective group (personal communication by a psychosocial helper). It follows that traumata and suffering have to be explained in political categories and thus made comprehensible for survivors in order to faciliate coping and healing (cf. Becker 1992, p. 159).

5   The 'local turn'—A Way Out?

Practitioners have realized the 'monumental gap' between the promises of neoliberal peace and the experience of individuals and communities exposed to these policies. They experience that the reconstruction process is in the hands of international actors and local profiteers, and that pressing social and welfare problems are largely ignored. The liberal peace rhetoric of human rights and the rule of law more often than not eschews the daily survival struggles of ordinary people (cf. Richmond 2010, p. 25). Moreover, liberal peace does not exactly display a

---

Vietnam-veterans who had been defeated, were demoralized and shunned on their return home (cf. Pupavac 2002, p. 495).

success story: Studies have shown that around 50% of the regions which underwent reconstruction efforts on the basis of liberal peace programmes relapsed into violent conflict within about five years (cf. Collier 2003, p. 83).

The so-called 'local turn' in peacebuilding and post-war reconstruction has been discussed as a possible way out of the liberal peace quandary. One of the first authors promoting a 'local turn' was John Paul Lederach who, in his seminal work on 'building peace' (Lederach 1998), presented a theory which moved peacebuilding away from 'high politics' or a 'governance approach', thus emphasizing the significance of doing work in what he called the mid-level and the grassroots of post-conflict societies or communities. The mid-level refers to societal groups including ethnic or religious leaders, academics, intellectuals and NGOs that are not connected with formal government or oppositional political groups; grassroots refer to community developers, local health officials, refugee camp leaders and teachers, i.e. local spokespeople who represent the a majority of the population and are in close contact with day-to-day problems in a post-war setting (ibid). For Lederach, post-war reconstruction is to follow a multi-track pathway moving the emphasis from state-building towards relationship building and supporting reconciliatory social dynamics at the grassroots. By rebuilding relationships between people that had been shattered by violent conflict, Lederach aimed at changes on personal, structural, relational and cultural levels, thereby attempting to bring about social change and social justice that would guarantee sustainable peace beyond the immediate post-conflict period (cf. Lederach 1998). This agenda not only indicates a turn towards the local in the peacebuilding discourse; it describes a field of activity that moves social work close to peacebuilding activities. Lederach's approach also evokes values that are akin to objectives of social work as presented by the international professional associations, thus laying a foundation for an exchange between social work and peace and conflict research.

The local turn has been seen as an opportunity to remedy the shortcomings of post-war reconstruction under liberal auspices and provide a source of resistance to the neoliberal project on local levels.

However, as experience with post-war reconstruction accumulated, the 'local' turned out to be more tricky and complex than anticipated. Firstly, there is no consensus on what 'the local' in post-conflict settings is. Indeed, there are multiple ways to define it, ranging from a specific geographical space to a network of actors. These actors may be local communities but also local governments or local elites (cf. Donais 2012, p. 10). Moreover, local communities in post-conflict situations are often deeply divided. Indeed, 'the local' is heterogenous and diffuse and not an obvious category. As Pfaffenholz has pointed out, although debates about the 'local turn' make important contributions to peace and conflict studies, the concept cannot be considered an easy remedy as 'the local' is not politically innocuous: It is fraught with power relations of various kinds, there is a vast diversity of local actors with various interests, and often an elite co-opts the reconstruction process. In the wake of this, there are various local responses to post-conflict reconstruction, ranging from acceptance to adapation, modification, resistance and rejection of liberal peace offers (cf. Pfaffenholz 2016, pp. 214).

Moreover, it is often overlooked that in a globalized world we are no longer dealing with *national* elites and/or profiteers. Instead, there has been a shift of power in that international elites and international post-conflict profiteers are now linked and pursue joint interests (cf. Taylor 2010, p. 155). The cooperation between local elites and individuals on the one hand, and international institutions on the other, serves the interests of both—privileging local elites and international actors while disadvantaging the bulk of the population. Often enough, this escapes attention (cf. ibid.). Domestic power structures thus often merge with international actors ' structures and can undermine the public good (cf. MacGinty in Debiel 2016, p. 207). Nordstrom convincingly describes how in war and post-war scenarios, we are dealing with a shadow economy that encompasses powerful local and international actors and produces war-zone profits of unprecedented dimensions (Nordstrom ibid., p. 235). Informal and semi-criminal economies are not a local phenomenon but a product of the cooperation of local and international profiteers making use of international extra-state networks. Nordstrom 's analyses of various war and post-war scenarios reveal that not only local elites profit from post-war shadow economies but also international elites who play a role in international, informal economies, establish links with humanitarian aid and routinely use globalized formal political networks to profit from 'the shadows of war' (Nordstrom 2004, pp. 10). Moreover, a large part of local activities will be economic interactions between local elites and outside 'conflict entrepreneurs' who jointly pursue interests such as the exploitation of natural resources, the sale of future resource exploitation rights, the capture of foreign aid or other licit and illicit economic activities (cf. Ballentine and Nitzschke 2005).

Yet the merging of the local and the international does not only take place in the pursuit of joint interests. The merging takes hold of society as a whole, modifying local and international mentalities. Keeping in mind that due to the financial power involved, 'the international' will occupy a hegemonic position with international actors generally having more power and exerting more influence than local ones, attention should be directed to the constant negotiations between local and international actors, and what has been called the 'hybrid', and, in a Foucauldian sense, the unpredictable outcomes of these developments (cf. Richmond 2009; McGinty 2016; Pfaffenholz 2018). For social workers, the message is: While cultural and ethnological knowledge becomes increasingly indispensable for work in this field, and while familiarity with and appreciation of local/indigenous knowledge and practices are part of social work professionalism, the hybrid space they occupy in post-conflict regions should caution practitioners not to romanticize indigenous practices or local actors as authentic sites of pure and politically innocuous practical knowledge (cf. Maglajic and Stubbs 2018).

Finally, a problem should be addressed which, from an international perspective, is often decried as clientelism and corruption in post-war regions, and which is often attributed to 'local customs'. It is not to be contested that cultural mores and local structures may be harmful to a democratic development and that 'the local' plays its role in the powermongering going on in reconstruction areas. However, there is some cultural essentialism involved in these allegations and a tendency to blame cultural influences and shortcomings for failures on a policy level that include more often than not international actors and profiteers (cf. Becirovic/Dowling cit in Majglajic and Stubbs 2018, p. 49).

In addition, we would be well advised to investigate the social conditions in which these acts are embedded: Particularly when we talk about corruption in the lower echelons of society, what deserves attention are the typical characteristics of societies that are particularly susceptible to such corruption: In virtually all such settings we can observe tremendous levels of social inequality as well as exceptional levels of social hardship and a 'survival economy'. As Pugh has poined out, in the welfare vacuum so characteristic of post-conflict settings, clientelism and corruption at the grassroots fill a welfare void for deprived sections of the population and can hardly be tackled by policy measures and moral pleas (cf. Pugh 2011, p. 472). Emphasis on the often-overlooked international involvement is not to diminish the responsibility of local elites: They often operate through patron-client relationships, in which elite circles secure their power by distributing favours and resources top-down in exchange for acquiescence and loyalty at the grassroots. However, in a 'coping economy' (cf. OECD 2012, p. 17), where it is necessary to engage in all kinds of informal activities to sustain a livelihood, it is not surprising that these offers are readily accepted by large parts of the population.

Finally, it has been observed that ultimately, international actors in liberal peace are not as concerned about corruption as the public rhetoric about the 'rule of law' might make us believe. Liberal peacebuilding is more interested in market access than anti-corruption and tolerates corruption 'if it fosters the right kind of stability in the eyes of Western donors and institutions' (Harvey 2012). Moreover, as empirical evidence shows, international liberal peace actors do not tend to shy away from reinforcing corrupt local elites and siphoning off privatised public assets (which more often than not requires bribing local elites), or the general encouragement of a mentality of greed that comes in the wake of a neoliberal society (cf. ibid).

6 Outlook

Social work is involved in armed conflict in various ways: As social work in postwar reconstruction, as refugee work, but also as military social work—a topic that has not been touched on here (cf. instead Seifert 2018). Postwar reconstruction and refugee work are caught up in conflicting demands and have to toe the line between the self-understanding of social work as a 'human rights profession' as expressed by associations such as the International Federation of Social Workers and the International Association of Schools of Social Work on the one hand, and on the other hand political demands and pressures which cannot be eschewed although they more often than not run counter to this self-definition. Social work dealing with the consequences of armed conflict is navigating a minefield of theoretical and practical issues and quandaries. In the practical realm, there are no set procedures and methods that can be recommended, and 'best practice' manuals with 'one size fits all' recommendations that reduce social work to the application of methods will be of little help. Social workers will be exposed to conflicting demands and exigencies and will have to deal with them. Given the theoretical and practical contradictions, dilemmas and paradoxes, the best way to handle the situation might be a kind of flexible guerilla tactic: analyze the situation contextually, act according to the options at a certain point in time, and be aware of the fact that actions might be theoretically wrong, but politically and practically the only alternative in a given situation. The local is not per se working towards the common good, and indigenous knowledge is not per se superior; at the same time, the international is not per se exploitative and colonial (cf. Pfaffenholz 2018, p. 221). Finding one's way through this maze will require social workers in the field to have empirical knowledge of the situation on the ground, of theoretical concepts that help them to understand the empirical findings, as well as knowledge of international politics and its contents and discontents.

References

Adams, G., Estrada-Villalta, S., Sullivan, D., & Markus, H. R. (Eds.) (2019). The psychology of neoliberalism and the neoliberalism of psychology. *Journal of Social Issues*, March 2019, 75(1), 189–216.

Alice-Salomon-Hochschule (2016). *Position Paper. Social Work with Refugees in Refugee Accommodation Centers*, Berlin.

Ballentine, K., & Nitzschke, H. (2005). *The Political economy of civil war and conflict transformation*. Berlin: Berghof Research Center for Constructive Conflict Management.

Becker, D. (1992). *Ohne Hass keine Versöhnung. Das Trauma der Verfolgten*. Freiburg: Kore Verlag.

Becker, D. (2014). *Die Erfindung des Traumas. Verflochtene Geschichten*. Gießen: Psychosozial Verlag.

Beristain, C. M. (2006). *Humanitarian aid work. A critical approach*. Philadelphia: University of Pennsylvania Press.

Bettelheim, B. (1990). *Erziehung zum Überleben. Zur Psychologie der Extremsituation*. München: dtv.

Chassé, K. A., et al. (2014). Re-Politisierung der Sozialen Arbeit? In B. Bütow (Ed.), *Das Politische im Sozialen. Historische Linien und aktuelle Herausforderungen der Sozialen Arbeit* (pp. 83–108). Stuttgart: Barbara Budrich Verlag.

Collier, P. (2003). *Breaking the conflict trap: Civil war and development policy*. Oxford: Oxford University Press.

Couturier, D. (2012). The rape of men: Eschewing myths of sexual violence in wars. In *On Politics*, ISSN Online, University of Victoria, B.S.: https://journal.uvic.ca/index.php/onpolitics/article/view/127770/5965.

Debiel, T., et al. (Eds.). (2016). *Peacebuilding in Crisis. Rethinking paradigms and practices of transational cooperation*. London: Routledge.

Dolan, C. (2014). *Into the mainstream: Adressing sexual violence against men and boys in conflict,* Workshop held at the Overseas Development Institute, London May 14th.

Donais, T. (2012). *Peacebuilding and local ownership: Post-conflict consensus-building*. London: Routledge.

Duffield, M. (2001). *Global governance and the new wars. The merging of development and security*. London: Zed Books.

Duffield, M. (2007). *Development, security and unending war. Governing the world of peoples*. Canbridge: Polity Press.

Filsinger, D. (2017). *Soziale Arbeit mit Flüchtlingen. Strukturen, Konzepte und Perspektiven*. Wiso Diskurs 14. Bonn: Friedrich-Ebert-Stiftung.

Harvey, K. (2012). What makes post-conflict situations particularly susceptible to corruption? E-International Relations Students: https://www.e-ir.info/2012/10/09/what-makes-post-conflict-situations-particularly-susceptible-to-corruption/.

Kafula, S. C. (2016). The role of social work in peace, Human rights, and development in Africa. *Journal of Education and Social Policy, 3*(5).

Kessl, F., & Hans-Uwe, O. (2012). Soziale Arbeit. In G. Albrecht & A. Gronemeyer (Eds.), *Handbuch sozialer Probleme*. Berlin: Springer VS.

Kessl, F. (2013). *Soziale Arbeit in der Transformation des Sozialen.* Berlin: Springer.
Kidd, S., *Pro-Poor or Anti-Poor? The World Bank and IMF's Approach to Social Protection.* www.cadtm.org/Pro-poor-or-anti-poor-The-World.
Lambach, D. (2014). Das veränderte Gesicht innerstaatlicher Konflikt. Internet-Dossier, Bundeszentrale für politische Bildung, https://www.bpb.de/internationales/weltweit/innerstaatliche-konflikte/54556/veraenderte-konflikte.
Lavalette, M., & Ioakimidis, V. (Eds.). (2011). *Social Work in extremis. Lessons for social work internationally.* Bristol: Policy Press.
Luci, N. (2004). Das 'Schweigen der Frauen': Genderkonstruktionen und Genderdynamiken im Vor- und Nachkriegs-Kosova. In R. Seifert (Ed.), *Gender, Identität und kriegerischer Konflikt. Das Beispiel des ehemaligen Jugoslawien* (pp. 152–170). Münster: Lit Verlag.
Maglajlic, R. A. (2011). International organisations, social work and war: A Frog's perspective reflection on the bird's eye view. In: Lavalette, M. & Ioakimidis, V. (eds.). (pp. 105–114).
Maglajlic, R. A., & Stubbs, P. (2018). Occupying liminal spaces in post-conflict social welfare reform? Local professionals and international organisations in Bosnia and Herzegovina. *British Journal of Social Work, 48,* 37–53.
Marthinsen, E., et al. (2019). Social work and neoliberalism: The trondheim papers. *European Journal of Social Work, 2,* 183–187.
McGinty, R. (2016). What do we mean when we use the term 'Local'? Imagining and framing the local and the international in relation to peace and order. In Debiel, T. et al. (eds.). (pp. 193–209).
Merk, U. (2001). Schnelle Eingreiftruppe Seele. Oder was ist kontextuell angepasste psychosoziale Arbeit? *Die Gewalt überleben. Psychosoziale Arbeit im Kontext von Krieg, Diktatur und Armut. Medico Report, 23,* 2–8.
Mlodoch, K. (2017). *Gewalt, Flucht—Trauma? Grundlagen und Kontroversen der psychologischen Traumaforschung.* Göttingen: Vandenhoeck & Ruprecht.
Münkler, H. (2002). *Die neuen Kriege.* Hamburg: Rowohlt.
National Association of Social Workers. (2016). www.socialworkers.org/practice/military/schoolsofsocialwork.asp.
Nordstrom, C. (2004). *Shadows of war: Violence, power, and international profiteering in the 21st century.* Oakland: University of California Press.
OECD. (2012). International drivers of corruption. A tool for analysis. https://www.oecd.org/corruption-integrity/reports/international-drivers-of-corruption-9789264167513-en.html.
Pfaffenholz, T. (2016). Peacebuilding goes local and the local goes peacebuildng. Conceptual discourses and empirical realities of the local turn in peacebuilding. In: Debiel, T. et al. (eds.), (pp. 210–226).
Pugh, M., et al. (Eds.). (2011). *Whose peace? Critical perspectives on the political economy of peacebuilding.* London: Palgrave Mcmillan.
Pupavac, V. (2001). Therapeutic governance: the politics of psychosocial intervention and trauma risk management. *Disasters, 25*(4), 358–372.
Pupavac, V. (2002). Pathologizing Populations and colonizing minds: International psychosocial programs in Kosovo. *Alternatives, 27,* 489–511.
Richmond, O. P. (2009). Liberal peace transitions: a rethink is urgent. In: Open Democracy Nov 19, 2009, https://www.opendemocracy.net/en/liberal-peace-transitions-rethink-is-urgent/.

Rieber, R. W., & Kelly, R. J. (1991). Substance and shadow: Images of the enemy, In Riebert, R. W. (eds.), *The psychology of war and peace: The image of the enemy* (pp. 3–38). Plenum Press.

Roberts, A. (2010). Lives and statistics: Are 90% of war victims civilians? *Survival, 52*(3), 115–136.

Rogers, O. W. (2008). Social work and the international humanitarian law: Rights, roles and responsibilities. *Journal of Social Work Ethics and Values, 5*(2), 82–97, https://jswve.org/download/2008-2/JSWVE-Fall-2008-Complete.pdf.

Schellhaas, C., & Seegers, A. (2009). Peacebuilding: imperialism's new disguise? *African Security Review, 18*(2), 1–15.

Seifert, R. (2018). Armed conflict and social work. In L. Wagner et al. (Eds.), *Handbuch Internationale Soziale Arbeit. Dimensionen—Konflikte—Positionen* (pp. 181–193). Weinheim: Beltz.

Selby, J. (2013). The myth of liberal peace-building. *Journal of Conflict. Security and Development, 13*(1), 57–86.

Semigina, T., & Gusak, N. (2015). Armed conflict in Ukraine and social work response to it: What strategies should be used for internally displaced persons? *Social, Health, and Communication Studies Journal, 2*(1), 1–24.

Slim, H. (2008). Killing civilians. Method, madness and morality in war. Columbia University Press.

Spolander, G., et al. (2014). The implications of neoliberalism for social work: A six-country international research collaboration. *International Social Work, 4,* 301–312.

Strauss, A., & Lutz, R. (2016). International social work. Working Paper no. 3. University of Applied Sciences, Jena.

Streeck, W. (2011). The crisis of democratic capitalism. New Left Review 71.

Taylor, I. (2010). Liberal peace, liberal imperialism: A Gramscian Critique. In O. Richmond (Ed.), *Peacebuilding* (pp. 154–174). Basingstoke: Palgrave.

Tonkens, E. (2019). Democratizing social work: From New Public Management to Democratic Professionalism: https://www.researchgate.net/publication/270451501.

Turshen, M. (2019). Violence against women in new war economies. In Zipfel, G. et al. (eds.), (pp. 73–92). Zubaan Publishers: New Dehli.

Webb, S. A. (2000). The politics of social work: Power and subjectivity. *Critical Social Work. An Interdisciplinary Journal Dedicated to Social Justice,* 1–2.

Yesufu, A. (2006). A peace paradigm for social work. In: Socialist Studies/Études Socialistes, Fall 2006.

Zipfel, G., Mühlhäuser, R., & Campbell, K. (Eds.). (2019). *In plain sight sexual violence in armed conflict.* Neu Dehli: Zubaan Publishers.

International Social Work and the Global Social Work Statement of Ethical Principles

Kristin Sonnenberg

Abstract

With continuing social problems all over the world, conflicts, crisis and war, it is important to ask how social work can address social problems, and to have a discourse at the local and global level about its tasks and aims. This is interlinked with the issues of a shared value base and a shared understanding of the education of professionals. At the international level, three main associations of social work play an important role in shaping a global understanding and possible agreement. They will be introduced briefly within their historical context and with examples of their current work. Under the umbrella organisation of the International Federation of Social Workers (IFSW), by October 2019 178 social work associations around the world had already agreed on the *Global Definition of Social Work* (IFSW and IASSW 2014) and the *Global Social Work Statement of Ethical Principles* (IFSW and IASSW 2018). The assumption is that these agreements and the underlying shared values and standards can strengthen the professional status of social workers at the global and local level. Therefore, different approaches towards social work ethics and possible functions of an ethical code are introduced. Finally, possible implications for international social work, and possible applications of universal principles in different local and cultural circumstances, are discussed.

K. Sonnenberg (✉)
Protestant University of Applied Sciences, Bochum, Deutschland
E-Mail: sonnenberg@evh-bochum.de

Keywords

International social work • Social work • Global professional standards • Ethical values • Ethical principles • Reflection • Attitude

1 Introduction

Professionalizing social work has been one of the aims researchers and practitioners have been pursuing since its very beginning. Strengthening the profession is currently a central task for communities of social workers all over the world. It is still an important issue in Germany, even after a history of around 150 years of professionalizing practice and 50 years of academic discourse. In other countries, professionalization is a new and arising question. This is particularly prevalent in countries like Iraqi-Kurdistan that are faced with reconstruction after crisis, conflicts, war or transformation. In Iraqi-Kurdistan, a milestone in the professional development of social work, in the sense of academic education, has been the newly introduced BA Social Work studies at Sulaimani University in 2014. In 2019, with the graduation of the first two cohorts, around 100 social workers have completed their education. During an international cooperation process, this admirable and successful pioneering work could be witnessed and experienced due to the joint work of the Protestant University of Applied Sciences in Bochum and the University of Sulaimani.

For academics and professionals, the International Federation of Social Workers (IFSW) introduced a regular process for exchange and discourse about the professionalization of social work at a global level. This makes it possible to integrate new developments and discourses within shared documents and statements at an international level and from different (local) contexts. The last version was published in 2014. The second meaningful document is the *Global Social Work Statement of Ethical Principles* (IFSW and IASSW 2018). This statement takes as its point of departure the *Global Definition of Social Work* (IFSW and IASSW 2014).

At a global level there are different approaches and developments to establish a professional status and identity. The aim of this contribution is to discuss:

- how the community of social workers can strengthen its professional status at a global and local level with agreed and shared values and standards,
- what function shared values and standards could have to establish a common professional ground,

- why this has to be a stable fundament on the one hand, while on the other hand flexibility is needed to change within time, context and places, and
- which implications might follow for international social work, especially within cooperative projects.

There are two levels where ethical principles are applied as guidance and framing concepts: The educational level within social work studies and the practical level for reflection of social work practice. In 2018, the Global Social Work Statement of Ethical Principles was updated. Some aspects of this framework will be used for a brief analysis of the question if and how these can be referred to as a guidance within the field of international social work (e.g. in cooperative projects) and in national or local contexts. In everyday work, there can be a range of different professions involved in social work, and the question arises how to balance universal standards and local conditions and variations. Finally, the influence this has on (new) arising social work professions, or on re-establishing them after crises and conflicts, is analysed.

2 Frameworks that May Strengthen the Social Work Profession

To start with, the latest version of the global definition, which was approved by the IFSW General Meeting and the IASSW General Assembly in July 2014, outlines the social profession's core mandates and the theoretical framework underpinning social work:

> 'Social work is a practice-based profession and an academic discipline that promotes social change and development, social cohesion, and the empowerment and liberation of people. Principles of social justice, human rights, collective responsibility and respect for diversities are central to social work. Underpinned by theories of social work, social sciences, humanities and indigenous knowledge, social work engages people and structures to address life challenges and enhance wellbeing.' (IFSW and IASSW 2014)

Following this definition, the social work profession's core mandates include promoting social change, social development, social cohesion, and the empowerment and liberation of people. The overarching principles of social work are: respecting the inherent worth and dignity of human beings, doing no harm, respecting diversity, and upholding human rights and social justice.

Advocating and upholding human rights and social justice is the motivation and justification for social work. The social work profession recognizes that human rights need to coexist alongside collective responsibility. The idea of collective responsibility highlights the reality that individual human rights can only be realized on a day-to-day basis if people take responsibility for each other and their environment. As laid down in the Global Social Work Statement of Ethical Principles it is important to create reciprocal relationships within communities (cf. IASSW 2018). Therefore, a major focus of social work is to advocate for the rights of people on all levels, and to facilitate outcomes where people take responsibility for each other's wellbeing and realize and respect the interdependence among people as well as between people and their environment.

Furthermore, the beginning of the definition by the IASSW and IFSW reflects an actual theoretical discourse within scientific communities about shaping the term 'social work'. Social workers and social work scientists argue that social work has to be accepted as an independent applied science, with the status of a discipline. This leads to the understanding of social work as a profession in the sense of a scientific or academic discipline, rather than being purely applied, practical, social work. This theoretical discourse invites reflection on professional identity. Part of it is a clarification of the role of social work compared to other sciences that are needed in education and practice to establish an interdisciplinary approach. In order to discuss this at an international level, it might be necessary to include a broader definition of social work, without neglecting specific professional standards as laid down in the *Global Standards for Social Work Education and Training* (IASSW and IFSW 2004). The current version of this document was adopted at the IASSW and IFSW General Assemblies in Adelaide, Australia in 2004. Over the last fifteen years, this document has served as an aspirational guide setting out the requirements for excellence in social work education.

3   A Historical Approach to Associations of International Social Work

To show the role of international approaches within social work, and to understand their origins, it is valuable to look back into the history of the international associations of social work and their efforts concerning a professional status and their aim of social change. This history shows that, from its beginning approximately 150 years ago, the development of social work can be described with an international perspective. The three main associations of international social work represent the framework that strengthens the social work profession worldwide, and they coordinate and publish global statements. In 1856, first steps of exchange were taken with the first congress in Brussels, which focused on social questions. In 1898 and 1901, around the turn of the century, the first comparable studies about poverty were conducted (Kruse 2009, p. 16 in Straub 2018, p. 22). As a starting point for professional and institutionalized exchange, networking and cooperation, the year 1928 is meaningful and therefore often named and discussed in the literature (for example Straub 2018, p. 23; Friesenhahn and Kniephoff-Knebel 2011, pp. 103). As a result of the Paris International Exposition and World Congress, the three central associations of international social work – or their precursor organizations – were founded: the International Federation of Social Workers (IFSW), the International Council of Social Welfare (ICSW) and the International Association of Schools of Social Work (IASSW).

These interlinked roots become immediately apparent in the first paragraph of the IASSW's description of their own history:

> 'The International Association of Schools of Social Work (IASSW) is the worldwide organization of schools of social work and educators. It has represented the interests of social work education and the values of the profession globally for nearly 90 years. IASSW was initiated at the first International Conference of Social Work, held in Paris in 1928. This landmark gathering, attended by over 2400 delegates from 42 countries, also resulted in the establishment of two partner organizations, the International Council on Social Welfare (ICSW) and the International Federation of Social Workers (IFSW). In 1929, the first president, Alice Salomon, led an organizational meeting in Berlin; at this early meeting, seven European countries along with the International Labour Organization (ILO) were represented. Participants agreed that the organization's purpose was to encourage the exchange of ideas and information, documentation of social work education, and organization of international conferences and seminars. These remain key purposes along with others.' (IASSW 2020)

A clear focus of IASSW, besides exchanging ideas and information, documentation of educational concepts and organizing international conferences, is aiming at cooperation of university staff and students. From the 1950s onwards, following the first congress after World War II in Paris, a phase of organizing conferences outside of Europe started. That meant including former colonized countries. Not until 2004, 76 years after its foundation, the first president from outside the Global North, in this case from Ethiopia, was elected (Straub 2018, pp. 24). National members from the respective countries are the Universities (for Applied Sciences) with Social Work Studies and Schools of Social Work. Current controversies are value dilemmas, diversity within social work and debates about the Global Agenda for Social Work and Social Development.

At its core, the International Council of Social Welfare is focused on developmental matters. As a non-governmental organization its tasks are: '(…) advocacy, knowledge-building and technical assistance projects in various areas of social development carried out at the country level and internationally (…)' (ICSW 2020). The documentation of 90 years of history highlights the ICSW's focus on social practice and transnational advocacy. Since the 1980s, a more substantial involvement of the Global South can be observed with a stronger focus on the Development Movements, promoting social development, and an interdisciplinary orientation which means nonprofessionals within the field of social work and social welfare can be included (Straub 2018, p. 26).

The IFSW is the federation where social workers from all over the world promote social justice, human rights and social development. One aim is to strengthen the profession at an international level. This is, for example, done through critical papers that focus on (socio-) political topics. Another task is to mandate the profession with legal representation. Furthermore, there is a strong link with human rights. During the professionalization of social work after World War II in 1945, and especially since the Helsinki conference in 1968, Human Rights have been a strong reference point for the profession of social workers and its mandate (Staub-Bernasconi 2019, p. 9). There are three dimensions included: a legal, an ethical and a professional-political dimension, which means an action-based theory.[1]

Whilst at the beginning the IFSW was founded by representatives from the Global North, the Global South is now very well represented (Wagner and Lutz 2018, p. 13). The structure of regions is aligned with the continents: Africa, Asia and Pacific, Latin America and Caribbean, Europe and North America. Since 1957, the association has focused on topics related to ethics and ethical principles (see Straub 2018, p. 25 referring to Healy and Hall 2009, p. 245).

In the 1950s, the journal *International Social Work* (IFSW 2020) was founded to strengthen scientific exchange. It is the official journal of the three main international social work associations IASSW, ICSW and IFSW. Abstracts of articles are translated into French, Spanish, Russian, Chinese and Arabic.

4   Current Topics and Status of International Social Work Associations

A good overview over current topics can be found in concrete statements, such as *Ethics in Social Work, Statement of Principles* (2018), recently revised at the

---

[1] The original German terms are *professionspolitisch* and *handlungstheoretisch*.

World Conference in Dublin 2018, and the *Global Standards for Social Work Education and Training of the Social Work Profession* (2004). The latter, which covers aims and guidelines for universities, was expected to be revised in 2020, because a revision every ten years is planned. With these developments a change of paradigms can be reconstructed. The revision of the *Global Definition of Social Work* in 2014, for example, represents the discussion concerning conflicts within the context of post-colonialism and globalization. Social cohesion, social development and indigenous knowledge have been integrated in the definition. Straub describes the process of integrating these aspects in the definition as gaining more diversity at a global level (Straub 2018, p. 27). These statements have considerable influence, given that all three associations have a consultative/advisory status at United Nations bodies, for example the World Health Organization, WHO, and die UN Refugee Agency UNHCR.

Global Social Work Conferences are conducted on a regular basis. For 2020, it was planned to host the conference in Canada. One aim of this conference has been to finalize the global consultation process that has been taking place over the past few years. As a result, the scientific committee has distilled 14 themes as starting points for discussion to collaborate on the *Global Social Work Agenda: 2020–30* (SWSD 2020). The aim is to set strategic priorities for the social work profession for a period of 10 years. At the moment these are:

- Sustainable Development Goals
- Indigenous Communities: Knowledge and rights
- Strengthening Communities
- Economic Development: Distribution of wealth and inequality
- Environmental Justice
- Social and Human Rights
- Sexual and Gender Diversity: Community, Practice and Rights
- Gender Rights: Different Identities
- Social Movements and Democracy
- Responses to Migration and Displaced Persons
- Social Protection Systems

Due to the current Covid-19 global pandemic, the latest conference was cancelled and changed into an online virtual conference, which took place from Fifteenth until Nineteenth of July 2020. The members of the conference discussed co-building social transformation as part of a global conversation about the future of social work. As the results of these discussions are unknown at the time of writing, examples from the past and other processes are drawn on to show how the aim of strengthening the professional status is realized. This includes possibilities for building a stronger voice and a political mandate of social work, such as (Straub 2018, p. 29):

- The World Social Work Day, which was established in 1983. There are worldwide celebrations on every third Tuesday in March.
- As a joint strategy to strengthen political influence, the *Global Agenda for Social Work and Social Development* from 2010–2020 is referring to the UN Millennium Development Goals (MDG) and the Sustainable Development Goals (SDG) Agenda 2030.
- Reports of the IASSW embrace good examples from teaching and practice. At the moment the aim is to include practitioners in research and integrate addressees of social work in teaching.

The World Social Work Day, '(…) is the key day in the year that social workers worldwide stand together to advance our common message globally' (IFSW 2020). In accordance with the Global Agenda, in the years 2019 and 2020 that day has highlighted the topic *Promoting the Importance of Human Relationships*: 'This theme was established to build international focus on the interdependence of people and the need for change in policies and social service delivery' (ibid.). In addition to this, IFSW Secretary-General Rory Truell commented on the theme as follows:

> '(…) This theme highlights that co-determining relationships between people, communities, nations are essential in addressing the social, economic and ecological challenges. Drawing on the core skills of bringing people together to balance needs in celebrated diversity, social work has a significant and essential contribution to make in every society. Our task and mission at the time is to advance this message in our communities, in our workplaces and with our governments and shape a sustainable future.' (Truell 2020)

In 2019, he focused on a comparison with the following words:

> 'There was a famous moment in recent history when politician Margaret Thatcher ushered-in the current global period of conservatism and the dismantling of state services when announcing: *there's no such thing as society, there are individual men and women*. Thatcher's view continues to have devastating effects as it remains dominant over many aspects of world and national politics. This 2019 World Social Work Day theme directly addresses this false and brutality conservative dogma. From the social work experience all people are bound together by social relationships that determine the quality and security of life. Worldwide the social work profession will unify in

promoting the importance of building policies and practices that recognize, cultivate and enrich our interdependent relationships – for peace, the realization of all people's equal rights and a sustainable world.' (Truell 2019)

This statement emphasizes a clear political mandate supported by basic social work ethical principles such as social rights and human dignity.

Taking both statements together, the following conclusions are important: Social work has to step back from individualized approaches (the so-called conservative dogma), but rather use a social relationship approach, because it has to be acknowledged that people live in interrelatedness. Solidarity in the sense of justice as fairness, equal rights, peace and sustainability are core values and aims. In his speech in 2020, Truell focuses on *co-determining relationships* and describes a holistic approach whilst integrating social, economic and ecological challenges into his considerations. He describes 'bringing people together to balance needs in celebrated diversity' as a core skill of social workers (Truell 2020), which leads to 'a significant and essential contribution to make in every society' (ibid.). This is an important suggestion for what it might mean to promote the importance of human relationships.

Another important conclusion with respect to social work ethical values and their meaning for international cooperation concerning social work is an approach that Banks calls *Progressive Social Work Ethics* or *A situated Ethics of Social Justice* (2012, p. 92). Banks suggests a situated ethics of social justice, which includes a set of values for progressive social work, based on Toronto's ideas of a political ethics of care. These focus on human relationships in the context of structures of power and oppression. As preliminary values for a situated ethics of social justice for social work, the following are central: radical social justice, empathic solidarity, relational autonomy, collective responsibility and moral courage (ibid., pp. 93).

Considering the complex contexts of social work that might be even more complex in international cooperation or projects, the progressive approach seems to be more flexible concerning situational and context-specific factors. At the same time, it sets basic non-negotiable principles and rules, such as social justice and human dignity. It encourages and demands exchange and discussion within teams and communities of social workers to reflect values and principles in specific contexts, and individual as well as social relationships with a focus on the moral agents in relation to their environment.[2]

---

[2] For further reading see: Sonnenberg 2021: Ethics and Ethical Values in Social Work and their meaning for International Social Work. In Ghaderi, C., Sonnenberg, K., Saleh Karim, L.,

5   Global Social Work Statement of Ethical Principles – Code of Ethics

A common form of putting agreed values into writing is a Code of Ethics. Most European countries, including for example Germany (DBSH[3] in 1974) and England (BASW[4] in 1975) introduced a code of ethics for social work. These codes are closely linked to the UN Convention of Human Rights and the Right of the Child, and later they were linked to the model of the International Federation of Social Work (IFSWs first version in 1976, see Baum 1996, p. 18). Codes can include values, general key principles, practice principles or even practical rules. The codes of BASW, NYA (British National Youth Agency) and IFSW have been criticized as very vague and as overly general (Banks 1995; Clark 1999; Shardlow 1998). Since its modification in 1997, the German Code has been more detailed (DBSH, 1999, p. 8). It is said to be very supportive and open to discourse in order to allow modification in case of changing values of society (Mühlum 1999). The nine principles of the IFSW 2018 version of the Global Social Work Statement of Ethical Principles are:

1. Dignity of Humanity
2. Human Rights
3. Social Justice
4. Right to self-determination
5. Right to participation
6. Confidentiality, privacy
7. People as whole persons
8. Technology and social media
9. Professional integrity

Within the discourse about a meaning and function of ethical codes, different interpretations and different functions of a code have been suggested (Banks 1995, pp. 73–89; Banks 1998, p. 221):

a) A code can help a profession to be recognised.

Namiq Sabir, N., Abbas Qader, Z., Dünnebacke, L.M. (Eds.). Social Work at the level of International Comparison. Examples from Iraqi-Kurdistan and Germany. Wiesbaden: Springer-VS. Forthcoming.

[3] DBSH = German Professional Association for Social Workers and Social Pedagogues.
[4] BASW = British Association of Social Work.

b) A code can maintain the professional identity by creating a sense of common identity and shared values.
c) A code can guide practitioners on how to act.
d) A code shall protect users from malpractice or abuse by professionals.

Concerning the first two interpretations, a code of ethics might help a profession to establish status and identity. The following guiding aspects protect clients and aim for good practice and self-confident practitioners. A code of ethics also encourages reflection. Within social work around the turn of the twenty-first century, a code was understood as a reference point for reflection, a 'map of the minefield of practice' (Payne 1996, p. 69) or as something fulfilling the 'function of a lighthouse' (Clark 1999, p. 259), serving as orientation and a warning of danger. However, it would not work out one's course, or destiny, since 'that is still a decision for the captain, which requires technical skills and moral judgment' (Clark 1999, p. 265). The perception of a code as a reference point or a lighthouse might lead to establishing clear and explicit definitions of the profession with respect to agreed ethical values. Codes could illuminate the issues and controversies of practical dilemmas, which is indispensable within the complex and ambiguous context of social work. Baum supports the idea of a general code, which would be based on fundamental world-concepts with ethical relevance and could be called 'universal solidarity' (Baum 1996, p. 111). He states that developing an ethical concept is evidence for high quality professionalism, and the duty of all professionals (ibid.). A shared responsibility and solidarity for each other within society and family or amongst friends is a core value for social work. Professional action should adjust to these values. The realization of the values responsibility and solidarity can follow at different levels as direct support, and it is not meant to be patronizing or humiliating.

To act responsibly in professional contexts there has to be a mandate either from the client, the state or the profession itself (Staub-Bernasconi 2007a; b). The ultimate responsibility for working at life-perspectives, searching for solutions and learning new strategies to cope with life rests with the persons concerned. If clients refuse help or cooperation, the social worker cannot take responsibility for that. An institution and the social workers can offer support, but not guarantee success. Ultimately, clients can decide to go their own way and take risks (Plattig 2003, p. 30).[5]

---

[5]Original quote: ‚Eine Institution kann fördern und helfen, sie kann aber nicht das Risiko des eigenen Weges übernehmen und sie kann keine Garantien geben.' (Plattig 2003, p. 30).

5.1 Members of IFSW and their Connection with the Code of Ethics

As of October 2019, 178 members in form of national associations of social workers were part of the IFSW. The five regions summarize their respective focus as follows:

- **Africa:** 'Social Work has a long history in Africa stemming back to pre-colonial times. The region now comprises 25 IFSW members who are working toward the establishment of a recognized social work profession association in all the region's countries, and the visibility of the profession's contributions in addressing the complex factors of poverty, HIV eradication, gender equality and self-led community empowerment.
- **Asia and Pacific:** Asia–Pacific is the most expansive IFSW region. It stretches from New Zealand in the south to the border of the Russian Federation, including the Middle East. The region focuses on social work responses to child trafficking, climate change, disaster recovery and societies in conflict.
- **Latin America and Caribbean:** LAC formed its own identity in the last fifty years. It has developed ideologically positioned theoretical skills, created methodologies that guide the specific practices of the social disciplines and has expressed a strong ethical-political commitment to the causes of the peoples of the region.
- **Europe:** This region covers all corners of Europe and represents IFSW at the EU, Council of Europe and at the UN centers in Geneva and Vienna. Social workers reframe austerity as a symptom of political crises. The region works with people affected by individual and family challenges, conflict, mass migration of people moving north, seeking safety and refuge from war and climate change.
- **North America:** CASW and NASW-USA are currently the two members of this region. Living in two different political environments they work together on strengthening the profession, addressing the de-professionalization of social work, recognizing the importance of research on evidence-based and best practices.' (IFSW 2020)

The Middle East is represented within the Asia and Pacific region. At the moment there are members from 28 countries, including six from the Middle East: Bahrain, Iran, Lebanon, Kuwait, Palestine and Yemen.

Out of the 178 members, the homepage lists 23 National Codes of Ethics of Social Work presented by IFSW Member organisations from the following countries (accessed 7th of October 2019): Australia, Canada, Denmark, Finland, France, Germany, Ireland, Israel, Italy, Japan, Luxembourg, Norway, Puerto Rico, Portugal, Russia, Singapore, South Korea, Spain, Sweden, Switzerland, Turkey, USA and United Kingdom. In general, they are written in the national languages of the different countries, and some are translated into English or another second language. More national codes of ethics are expected to follow in the future.

5.2 Social Work in Iraqi-Kurdistan – Ethical principles

To date, there is no association of social workers in Iraqi-Kurdistan. Instead, social workers tend to be members of the syndicates of psychologists or sociologists. Professional social work in Iraqi-Kurdistan has been in a pioneer phase since the introduction of social work studies in 2014/15 in Slemani. The first BA *Social Work*-studies in Iraqi-Kurdistan was established at the University of Salahadin in Erbil in 2008/09 (see Ghaderi and Saleh Karim 2019, p. 177). At other universities, social work is part of sociology, e.g. at the University of Dohuk (see UoD 2019). However, the practical fields, structure and regulation are growing. Since 2016, there have been initiatives that plan to establish a stronger network for the profession. At a conference organized by the US Agency for International Development, USAID, in Erbil in 2016, the International Code of Ethics from the IFSW was discussed. For the field of social work in prisons, Salah Sdiq Saed, Director of Access to Justice Program, Erbil Office, presented a paper with the title 'Social Researchers' Conduct Regulations in the Juvenile Judicial System'.[6] The conduct itself is described as:

> '(…) set of rules and guidelines of behaviors to regulate the relationship between social workers and juveniles.
>
> This is for the sake of commitment to the professional boundaries and best compliance by the social workers on one hand, and to ensure juveniles' rights and achieving the best interest of children in Kurdistan Region on the other.
>
> These regulations are not to identify the researchers' detail of daily work. They are rather some main principles to set the researchers' relationship especially in those fields where confrontations can be found between the researchers' values and culture and the cases they see.

---

[6]Paper prepared by Salah Sdiq Saed Director of Access to Justice Program, Erbil Office, 2016, unpublished pdf-version.

They are also to offer help for making decisions professionally in order to avoid conflict of interest. These regulations have made (to an extent) the main principles of universal declaration of children rights a source to deal with juveniles: which are children's best interest, desegregation, and involvement for the sake of survival and growth of children.' (Salah Sdiq Saed 2016, p. 1)

The conduct is defined as a set of rules, guidelines and main principles for orientation, rather than practical advice. It aims to help practitioners to make decisions in difficult situations, dilemma situations or ambiguous decision-making processes. Another aspect is the description of the relationship between professionals and their clients. It establishes a strong link with children's rights and the rights of juveniles in participating during the processes (UN-Children's Right Act 1989), and explicitly their survival. Salah Sdiq Saed continues to highlight the principles of social work – such as respecting and applying human rights principles and social justice, human integrity, professional skills and tangibility: 'Social researchers work in a moral and trustworthy manner and observe conduct principles of social work. At the same time they are aware of the influence of their personal values.' (Salah Sdiq Saed 2016, p. 2).

This conduct names the area of social work and mentions a specific practical field, but the active persons addressed are called 'the researchers' from the syndicate of sociologists, at universities, the Departments of Social Affairs, Sociology or Psychology. In 2016, social work as a distinct profession had not yet been listed, whereas the area of social work within the Juvenile Judicial System was already well defined. B.A. Social Workers can now start their working life in this area.

6 Implications for International Social Work

Healy offers a concise definition of international social work: '(…) *international social work* is defined as international professional action and the capacity for international action by the social work profession and its members' (2008, p. 10). International action comprises four dimensions: internationally related domestic practice and advocacy, professional exchange, international practice and international policy development and advocacy.

Within the scientific debate, an *integrated-perspectives approach* is discussed and recommended (Cox and Pawar 2013; Straub 2018). It covers current fields and debates where international social work should be involved. These include the diversity of the profession, the integration of human rights (e.g. values and principles), globalization (e.g. interdependence, global citizenship), ecology (e.g. sustainability) and social development (e.g. proactive intervention, multilevel). The model is described as 'multi-perspective' and can be applied to international social work practice (Friesenhahn and Kniephoff-Knebel 2011, pp. 98). As a consequence, international social work includes the aims of social change and development, social cohesion and the empowerment and liberation of people to improve their well-being. This has to be done by following the principles of social justice, human rights, collective responsibility and respect for diversities. International social work has the task of identifying diverse ways of living and bringing together various forms of knowledge (theories, indigenous approaches, narrative access), methods and practical field experience. It also has the task of highlighting conflicts within the current discourses about the reflection and reprocessing of (post)colonial influences, as well as new imbalances and unjust power relations.

6.1 The Meaning of Value-Based Action

A value-based attitude is the necessary foundation of professional action. The basic assumption here is: The inner will to reflect, and the ability to reflect critically, lead to a widening and reinforcement of social workers' competences to make decisions in their daily work, and handle conflicts and ethical dilemmas in the best possible way.

An important feature of values-based action are therefore the reflective skills of students, researchers and practitioners. Professional social work comprises expertise, practical competences and a professional attitude. The validation of one's own values or of the clients' value-base facilitate the competence of critical reflection. This may contribute to self-assurance and self-care. There is a wide range of values that can be referred to in the history of social work. These can be spirituality; the influences of Christian (or other religious) values such as belief, love and trust; humanistic values that contribute to an understanding of dialogue-based education and subjective interpretation of reality; justice and social responsibility and economic values as framing conditions.

Ethical standards or principles may change within historical contexts, and are based in certain societal circumstances. Therefore, an ongoing discussion and reflection about social work (ethical) values is necessary. The social workers themselves need this controversy as a basis for responsible action and for developing critical reflective skills and abilities. This is significant in two different ways: the personal level of self-assurance and self-care, and the development of a professional identity and professionalization. As a theoretical framework, the

Progressive Social Work Ethics or *A situated Ethics of Social Justice* (Banks 2012, p. 87*)* offers a valid approach that focuses on human relationships in the context of structures of power and oppression.

6.2 Social Justice and Responsibility as Core Values of (International) Social Work

From its beginning in Germany, Western Europe and North America, social work has had the task to promote social justice. In the early twentieth century Germany, Alice Salomon (1872–1948) wrote about social work and social justice. She was well connected internationally and worked with – amongst others – Jane Addams from North America. Salomon states that social injustice is the central cause for social problems. She demands societal solidarity and structural solutions such as distributional justice: 'Social work is based on the principle that the collectivism has to shoulder responsibility for the weak' (1930 cit. in Kuhlmann 2000, p. 223). She argues that collectivism is responsible for injustice, selfishness and recklessness deriving from so-called *social fights*. That means that society is responsible for creating the (unjust) conditions for living. These structural aspects may be access to resources, such as income, education, infrastructure, food and living conditions.

The most recent version of the Global Social Work Statement of Ethical Principles (2018) mentions the three core principles right at the start: Recognition of the Inherent Dignity of Humanity (1), Promoting Human Rights (2) and Promoting Social Justice (3). Regarding Human Rights, it states:

> '2.2 Social workers respect and defend the human rights principle of indivisibility, and promote all civil, political, economic, social, cultural and environmental rights.
>
> 2.3 Recognizing that culture sometimes serves as a disguise to violate human rights, social workers serve as cultural mediators to enable consensus building, find an appropriate balance between competing human rights, and to advocate for the rights of marginalized, stigmatized, excluded, exploited and oppressed individuals and groups of persons.
>
> 2.4 Social workers recognize that human rights need to coexist alongside collective responsibility, understanding that individual human rights can only be realized on a day-to-day basis if people take responsibility for each other and the environment, and if they work towards creating reciprocal relationships within communities.' (IFSW and IASSW 2018)

These lines clarify a clear political mandate based on a human rights perspective (2.2): not only a political mandate, but also a holistic approach, including social and cultural rights. However, there might be competing rights or cultural aspects that tend to challenge or violate human rights. In this case, social workers serve as cultural mediators to enable consensus building. To enable consensus building they advocate marginalized and stigmatized individuals or groups. While the aspect of being a cultural mediator is relatively new, the aspect of mandating the oppressed has always been inherent to social work. In social work practice, there are many challenges within differing cultural contexts and values, and it seems to be a necessary and significant aspect of international social work (2.3). The *collective responsibility and reciprocal relationships within communities* (2.4) are named as coexisting with human rights. In the context of international social work, the statement underlines respectful and reflective critical awareness at local levels, with regard to common global standards or orientation. The reciprocal idea of relationships is one approach that enables cooperation without power inequality in the sense that one partner might disempower the other. The idea is to work and cooperate at the same level with the same rights of participation.

6.3 Final remarks

To sum up, a shared value base can strengthen the profession in different ways: by providing guidance in difficult situations (conflicts, dilemmas), establishing professional status and identity at a global and local level, and by enabling and supporting reflective skills for high quality social work in accordance with human dignity and social justice. In practice, there has to be a way of integrating agreed standards and local conditions. This could be of special significance when social workers face a societal reality after a time of crisis, war or conflicts, where new forms of professionalized social work are needed or have to be reconstructed. The first steps are generally in approaching theory and methods that already exist. A second step is the critical reflection of these models and possibly their modification, adaptation or creation of methods and solutions that match the problems within their context. These two steps and the integration of international values and standards can help to professionalize social work. Two other articles in this book show and analyze practical examples of context-sensitive social work with special awareness for the affected people in need and their resources, strength and creativity in problem-solving as experts of their lives (see *Berenice Meintjes* and *Karin Mdlodoch*).

With respect to international cooperation and projects, sharing ideas about ethical values and guidelines can be a fruitful approach to reflect on social work in an international context. On the one hand, exchanging ideas and issues can widen our own understanding of difficult ethical decision-making, and on the other hand, it will strengthen an individual professional identity and attitude, which is a central part of professional thinking and acting. This international comparison might provide a common ground when different countries choose the same international values and principles such as the international definition of social work or the global ethics for a social work. An ethical background to reflect practice and cooperation within a range of professions in the social welfare field is seen as a universal good. How these universal principles may be applied in local and cultural circumstances is an important discourse and should be further discussed in the future.

References

Banks, S. (1995). *Ethics and values in social work*. London: Macmillan.
Banks, S. (1998). Professional ethics in social work – What future? *British Journal of Social Work, 28,* 213–231.
Banks, S. (2012). *Ethics and values in social work* (4th ed.). Palgrave: London.
Baum, H. (1996). *Ethik Sozialer Berufe. (Ethics of the social professions)*. München: Schöningh.
Clark, C. (1999). Observing the lighthouse. From theory to institutions in social work ethics. *European Journal of Social Work, 2*(3), 259–270.
Cox, D., & Pawar, M. (2013). *International social work. Issues, strategies, and programs* (2nd ed.). SAGE: Los Angeles.
DBSH. (ed.) (1999). *Stellenwert und Funktion der Sozialen Arbeit im Bewußtsein der Bevölkerung Deutschland. (Values/Significance and Function of Social Work in the German Public Consciousness)*. Essen: DBSH.
Friesenhahn, G., & Kniephoff-Knebel, A. (2011). *Europäische Dimensionen Sozialer Arbeit*. Schwalbach/TS: Wochenschau.
Ghaderi, C., & Luqman, S. K. (2019). Social work with refugees in Kurdistan region in Iraq. In M. Pfaller-Rott, A. Kallay, & D. Böhler (Eds.), *Social work with migrants and refugees* (pp. 163–185). Ostrava: University of Ostrava.
Healy, L. M. (2008). *International social work. Professional action in an interdependent world* (2nd ed.). New York: Oxford University Press.
IASSW. (2018). Global social work statement of ethical principles. https://www.ifsw.org/wp-content/uploads/2018/07/Global-Social-Work-Statement-of-Ethical-Principles-IASSW-27-April-2018-1.pdf. Accessed 11 October 2019.
IASSW. (2020). International Association of Schools of Social Work. A brief history. https://www.iassw-aiets.org/about-iassw/brief-history/. Accessed 17 July 2020.

ICSW. (2020). International Council on Social Welfare. About ICSW. https://www.icsw.org/index.php/about-icsw. Accessed 17 July 2020.

IFSW. (2020). International Federation of Social Workers. International social work. https://www.ifsw.org. Accessed 17 July 2020.

IASSW & IFSW. (2004). Global standards for social work education and training. https://www.iassw-aiets.org/global-standards-for-social-work-education-and-training/. Accessed 14 October 2019.

IFSW & IASSW. (2014). Global definition of social work. https://www.ifsw.org/what-is-social-work/global-definition-of-social-work/. Accessed 27 August 2019.

IFSW & IASSW. (2018). Global social work statement of ethical principles. Long version, 27.04.2018. https://www.ifsw.org/wp-content/uploads/2018/07/Global-Social-Work-Statement-of-Ethical-Principles-IASSW-27-April-2018-1.pdf. Accessed 27 August 2019.

Kuhlmann, C. (2000). *Alice Salomon: Ihr Lebenswerk als Beitrag zur Entwicklung der Theorie und Praxis sozialer Arbeit*. Weinheim: Deutscher Studienverlag.

Mühlum, A. (1999). Jahrestagung 1998: Das Ethos der Sozialen Arbeit in der Berufsbildung, Ausbildung und im Diskurs der Profession. (Annual conference 1998: The Ethos of Social Work in professional conduct, education and discouse). In DGS, Mitgliederrundbrief/Member Circular, April 1999, pp. 4–11.

Payne, M. (1996). *What is professional social work?* Birmingham: Venture Press.

Plattig, M. (2003). Was ist Spiritualität? In M. Lewkowicz & A. Lob-Hüdepohl (Eds.) *Spiritualität in der sozialen Arbeit* (pp. 12–32). Freiburg im Breisgau: Lambertus.

Salah Sdiq Saed. (2016). Social researchers' conduct regulations in the Juvenile Judicial System. Unpublished.

Shardlow, S. (1998). Values, Ethics and Social Work. In R. Adams, L. Dominelli, & M. Payne (Eds.), *Social Work* (pp. 23–33). Themes, Issues and Critical Debate.

Staub-Bernasconi, S. (2019). *Menschenwürde, Menschenrechte, Soziale Arbeit. Die Menschenrechte vom Kopf auf die Füße stellen*. Opladen: Verlag Barbara Budrich.

Staub-Bernasconi, S. (2007). *Soziale Arbeit als Handlungswissenschaft*. Bern: Verlag Haupt UTB.

Staub-Bernasconi, S. (2007). Vom beruflichen Doppel – Zum professionellen Tripelmandat. Wissenschaft und Menschenrechte als Begründungsbasis der Profession Soziale Arbeit. *Zeitschrift Für Sozialarbeit in Österreich (SiÖ), 1*, 10–36.

Straub, U. (2018). Definitionen Internationaler Sozialer Arbeit. In L. Wagner, R. Lutz, C. Rehklau, & F. Ross (Eds.), *Handbuch Internationale Soziale Arbeit. Dimensionen – Konflikte – Positionen* (pp. 22–34). Weinheim: Beltz Juventa.

SWSD. (2020). World Social World Day. Homepage. https://swsd2020.com/. Accessed 17 July 2020.

Truell, R. (2019). About SWSD 2019 at IFSW homepage. https://www.ifsw.org/social-work-action/world-social-work-day/world-social-work-day-2019/. Accessed 16 July 2020.

Truell, R. (2020). About SWSD 2020 at IFSW homepage. https://www.ifsw.org/social-work-action/world-social-work-day/world-social-work-day-2020/. Accessed 17 July 2020.

UoD, University of Duhok. (2019). Sociology. https://web.uod.ac/ac/c/coh/departments/sociology/. Accessed 3 May 2019.

Wagner, L., & Lutz, R. (2018). Internationale Soziale Arbeit zwischen Kolonialisierung und Befreiung. Eine Einleitung. In L. Wagner, R. Lutz, C. Rehklau, & F. Ross (Eds.), *Handbuch*

Internationale Soziale Arbeit. Dimensionen – Konflikte – Positionen (pp. 7–20). Weinheim: Beltz Juventa.

Knowledge Production in International Social Work – Postcolonial Perspectives

Nausikaa Schirilla

Abstract

In recent decades, concepts of international social work have been confronted with the idea that they were merely an export of western concepts. Thus, the international definition of social work has been changed in order to include indigenous knowledge as a principle of social work. Yet what can indigenous knowledge mean in a society where there is no tradition of social work? How can social work be adapted to specific local and cultural contexts? Are there barriers of thinking that hinder answering these questions? I will try to answer these questions from various viewpoints. I will present postcolonial conceptions, their critique and discuss consequences for knowledge production in social work.

Keywords

Epistemic violence · Postcolonial studies · Indigenous knowledge · International social work

A student of mine who was from the African state of Burundi and who studied in Germany always used to sigh loudly when I introduced new methods or approaches in social work. She used to say: 'Oh that sounds interesting, but I have to think of how we can apply these methods to my home country – the society there is so different, I do not think you can transfer all these good ideas one by one'.

N. Schirilla (✉)
Catholic University of Applied Sciences, Freiburg, Germany
E-Mail: nausikaa.schirilla@kh-freiburg.de

© The Author(s), under exclusive license to Springer Fachmedien Wiesbaden GmbH, part of Springer Nature 2021
K. Sonnenberg and C. Ghaderi (eds.), *Social Work in Post-War and Political Conflict Areas*, https://doi.org/10.1007/978-3-658-32060-7_4

Social work presents a profession that exists all over the world, due to its specific history and due to processes like globalization. Since the beginning of social work, but more strongly in recent decades, both social issues and the profession itself have spread internationally. One of the challenging issues concerning international social work is the question of which theories and approaches to apply or how to generate knowledge based on theories, approaches and methods that would be valid or applicable on a global level (Lutz und Rehklau 2007). Welfare systems, political circumstances, social organisation and cultural as well as academic traditions vary all over the world, so the context within which social work takes place might differ considerably. Many debates on the adequacy of 'western' knowledge discuss whether importing knowledge generated in western countries or in the Global North is adequate, or if it is rather important to ask if it is fitting or whether it is to be adapted. Also, in countries where social work as a discipline is quite new there are always particular mixtures in many areas; concepts are mostly adapted and particular regional traditions are founded (Lutz und Rehklau 2007).

Furthermore, taking into account that many countries in the so-called developing and developed world have experienced colonialism either as colonies or as colonizers, the question arises if social work knowledge represents an import of the North to the South and is thus an element of the colonial heritage. From a postcolonial perspective, contemporary international social work is equivalent to a new form of imperialism. According to that position, social work started as a profession of the Global North (or the West) and spread its theories and methods all over the world without examing if they were well-suited or not. Academic debates in social work in various parts of the world – both North and South – try to clarify which knowledge in social work practices, theories and knowledge can advance social work of the South, and they critique social work of the North whenever knowledge is exported to different countries without being adapted to different contexts.

On the other hand, social work can be perceived of as a global profession, based upon certain universal values and ethical orientations – as human rights and social justice – that are applicable everywhere regardless of the political, social or cultural context. If social work is perceived as a rather locally based profession that needs to be adapted to location-specific contexts like history, culture and religion, then questions arise concerning the universal orientation, as to how the universal or global principles remain unchanged.

Nowadays, social work is experiencing an increasing awareness of inequality in knowledge production and dissemination, and there are many debates about the extent to which the multiple contexts of social work bring multiple forms of knowledge to the fore (Pfaller-Rott et al 2018). Consequently, social work practitioners and theorists have followed the postcolonial movement of scholars and practitioners in a variety of disciplines, and are arguing forcefully for indigenous knowledge to be included in their search for new context-related knowledge. They argue for the development of truly indigenized and culturally appropriate social work knowledge that is free from the restrictions and expectations of western worldviews. In this contribution I argue for the importance of epistemic aspects of this movement. Firstly, I will show how indigenous knowledge was integrated into the international definition of social work. Secondly, I will show the theoretical background of the conceptionalization of indigenous knowledge in Latin American decolonial approaches, and thirdly I will stress the epistemic consequences and discuss concepts like epistemic violence. Finally, I will try to illustrate the practical side of these highly theoretical debates.

The quest for an adaptation or indigenization of knowledge in social work is reflected in the amendment of the international definition of social work from 2014, which adds 'indigenous knowledge' to the principles of social work. According to that definition, 'social work is a practice-based profession and an academic discipline that promotes social change and development, social cohesion, and the empowerment and liberation of people. Principles of social justice, human rights, collective responsibility and respect for diversities are central to social work. Underpinned by theories of social work, social sciences, humanities and indigenous knowledge, social work engages people and structures to address life challenges and enhance wellbeing.' (www.ifsw.org). In this definition, we find indigenous knowledge on the same level as science. Thus, local and autochthonous ideas and experiences regarding the social sphere, the challenges of social change and the human being are seen as a legitimate resource of social work interventions.

The new definition was followed by an amendment of the ethical principles of social work. In 2018, the international conference of the International Federation of Social Workers (IFSW) and the Association of Schools of Social Work passed the *Global Social Work Statement of Ethical Principles* in Dublin (wwww.isfsw.org). The statement of ethical principles is slightly different from the old ethical codex, which emphasized liberal humanist values common in the Global North. The new ethical statement is based on nine principles that rather reflect the global nature of the social work profession. It also mentions human dignity, human rights, diversity and social justice but adds discrimination, access to equitable resources, challenging unjust policies and building solidarity, the right to self-determination and the right to participation.

Considering these general statements, many questions arise concerning the topic of this volume. First, there is the question of how it is possible to pursue human dignity and rights in political conflict areas. What is the scope of social work as an intermediary institution in conflict situations? What kind of knowledge does social work produce or need in a post-conflict situation in colonialized societies? If we look at the Kurdish situation, we can even speak of a double colonization (Özbek 2011). What kind of knowledge does social work need in a double-colonized society?

In order to clarify what indigenous knowledge might mean in this context, I want to go back to the theoretical strands where indigenous knowledge plays an important part. In the Latin American context (although not only there), it is related to the perspective of 'decolonialisation of knowledge' (Mignolo 2012).

I refer to postcolonial or decolonial approaches by authors like Gayatri C. Spivak and Walter Mignolo. In general, authors who argue for taking into account colonial influences on global modern thought, and who come from an Indian and US American perspective, are referred to as 'postcolonial thinkers'. In contrast, authors arguing from a Latin American perspective are referred to as 'decolonial thinkers'. The main idea of both is that colonialism is related to a global matrix of power that is still at work in current times (Loomba 1998). This means that the influence of European ways of thinking is still dominant and shapes ways of thinking on the global level. Certain patterns of thought have shaped approaches to nature, to the world, to the social and the human all over the world, irrespective of cultures, religions and local traditions. Therefore, authors like Spivak or Mignolo speak of 'epistemic dominance' (Mignolo 2012; Spivak 1999). Although European knowledge is manifold and not unique, these authors refer to the most important and influential strands of European thought that dominated the representation of European thought and shapes thinking all over the world.

One of the outcomes of epistemic dominance according to these authors is the fact that European-based thinking ignored, degraded or destroyed alternative, traditional and indigenous ways of thinking in the former colonies. Traditional approaches were regarded as backward, uncivilized and unmodern (Davies 1993). This way of thinking is still prevalent today.

Decolonial authors like Anibal Qijano or Mignolo argue that there is a strong link between modernity, colonialism and domination. There are structural links between modern European thought and colonialism that lead to a general epistemic dominance of western thought in all countries of the world (Saal 2013).

Walter Mignolo puts it as the question of what counts as knowledge and what does not. Mignolo and other authors point to an epistemic hegemony in our thinking that leads to the exclusion of certain ways of thinking from being considered as knowledge at all, and to a degradation of non-western thought. For example, traditional or indigenous concepts of nature or the human being and other alternative discourses or thinking of marginalized groups were silenced (Qintero und Garbe 2013). Certains fields of thinking are strongly influenced by these patterns of thought that devalue indigenous thinking. They relate to ideas of person and personality or to the constitution of the subject in the sense that the free autonomous individual is seen as a subject or a person and that all other conceptions of the individual are marked as 'collective' or 'traditional'.

Another important field of thinking concerns the attitude towards the world that is based on the separation of the human and nature, or the separation of body and mind. Any thinking that is based on conceptions of an unseparable relationship between human beings and nature are marked as – for example – backward, or hostile to modernity and technology. Modern European knowledge thereby questions many religious and local traditions of thought.

As a consequence, Mignolo argues for decolonial options. He wants to open the mind for new forms of thinking and new forms of knowledge derived from local traditions, practices and experiences. Mignolo, amongst others, is looking for hidden knowledge and for subversive knowledge from local and indigenous traditions that were ignored by the global matrix of power (Tlostanova und Mignolo 2012). According to Mignolo and others, decolonial options of thinking are very often based on indigenous ideas on social cohesion and the relation to nature.

One of the examples Mignolo and his fellow thinkers mention are the world views of Indian communities in Latin America which are called 'buen vivir', and the ideas of social organization put into practice by the Zapatist revolution in the south of Mexico after 1994. The Zapatist movement reorganized local government structures and local economies in a collective way, based on traditional forms of organization of the local Indian communities. These traditional forms of collective organisation had until then been regarded as backward, unmodern and uncivilized. They had formed part of a general prejudice towards the Indian communities in Mexico and other Latin American countries (Vasquez 2012).

The main idea of these authors is to continuously put into question colonial influence on knowledge in order to aquire new forms of knowledge. Mignolo writes that we have to 'Learn to unlearn in order to relearn' (Tlostinova and Mignolo 2012). By this, he means that we have to question certain patterns of thought that form part of usual ways of thinking and do not take into consideration alternative ways of thinking or of social organization. In order to 'discover' the practical or emancipatory dimension of traditional ways of social organization, it is necessary to question colonial legacies in our knowledge. Mignolo calls these new perspectives – the outcome of 'Learning to unlearn in order to relearn' (Tlostanova and

Mignolo 2012, p. 1) – 'border thinking' and 'border epistemology' (ibid.). He encourages us to think beyond what counts as adequate knowledge (for him, this often means to overcome linear, instrumental and causal thinking), and to think beyond what seems to be thinkable. He questions prohibitions of thoughts and looks for what is barred from being taken into account. The aim is that those who are marginalized by the dominant patterns of knowledge production should produce their own knowledge, and that this knowledge – which might be based on traditions and religion – should not be called 'wisdom' or 'tradition', but rather 'knowledge'. So different kinds of knowledge would be regarded as actual knowledge, and this would suggest a diversification of knowledge. Although this raises new questions regarding the differences between knowledge, habits and tradition and the actual definition of knowledge, I think that this perspective can be very fruitful as it might open new ways of looking at hidden, traditional or lost elements of knowledge.

On the other hand, a very important objection to these ideas can be put forward from an emancipatory point of view. Local knowledge and its gatekeepers can be very oppressive, thus contributing to strengthening or legitimizing opression in general and oppression of women in particular, and obstructing change. One could argue that certain elements of local culture and dominant religious traditions contribute to the persistence of social problems and inequalities. In order to arrive at a more just and free society, some religious traditions must therefore be questioned. Modern European knowledge and values are directed against dominant local traditions, and so many human rights activists or women's rights activists liberate themselves from autochthonous traditions.

My point is not to argue that local or traditional knowledge or practices are always to be rediscovered and freed from colonial domination and my point is not that local knowledge is always good or adequate knowledge. The idea of Mignolo is to free thinking from epistemic dominance in the sense that what might be 'unthinkable' can be thought, that emancipatory elements of traditional approaches are used and taken up – that we free ourselves from taboos or prohibitions in our thinking. I am thinking of an example a Tunisian colleague once gave at a conference. She mentioned that in Tunisia, women always thought everything in traditional society was oppressive towards women and they had to imitate western culture in order to achieve gender equality. But then they discovered that in Arab traditions women could keep their names when marrying, whereas in some western countries women had to take the name of their husbands when marrying. Thus women were fighting exactly for an option that Arab women already had.

What do these approaches mean for social work? On the one hand, the 'decolonialisation of knowledge' demands that we reflect on knowledge transfer and knowledge production in order to identify exclusive scientific conceptions which mark knowledge production for social work as solely empirical and evidence-based. As a consequence, these ideas demand a certain modesty from academics – they cannot view themselves as the sole producers of knowledge and should develop sensitivity towards excluding practices in teaching and theory production. Similar issues are debated by antiracist authors, for example the author and artist Grada Kilomba always asks what is recognized as knowledge and who is allowed to produce knowledge (Kilomba 2008) and refers to marginalized groups affected by racial prejudices.

What does that mean for knowledge production in social work? It means to recognize practices, traditions, and philosophies that do not fit into the western body of knowledge for social work. An example is the idea of Ubuntu that is popular in certain regions of the African continent. In Ubuntu, there prevails an understanding of human beings foremost through their relationalities and embeddedness into a human community and not as individuals. This idea recognizes the importance and the strength of communities and uses the community as a resource to respond to challenges and to solve problems (Bimsbergen 2002). As Berenice Meintjes argues in this volume, this approach is used by the South African NGO Sinani as an element in healing post-trauma distress.

This is only one example, however what I want to argue for is to watch out for prohibitions of thinking and to look for new epistemic patterns, for alternative accounts of the human being and the social, for liberatory elements in local traditions. This quest means to question 'pure' imitations of western knowledge on the one hand, and to open up towards the variety of sources of knowledge production for social work in general. Finally, do we need a global dialogue on how to conceive of social cohesion referring to local traditions? How should we think about empowerment and the liberation of people by referring to different traditions? Knowledge production in societies all over the world will benefit from the answers to come.

References

Davies, M. W., Nandy, A., & Sardar, Z. (1993). *Barbaric others. A Manifesto on Western Racism.* London: Boulder.
Kilomba, G. (2008). *Plantation Memories.* Münster: Unrast.
Loomba, A. (1998). *Colonialism, Postcolonialism.* London: Routledge.
Mignolo, W. D. (2012). *Epistemischer Ungehorsam. Rhetorik der Moderne, Logik der Kolonialität und Grammatik der Dekolonialität.* Wien: Turia und Kant.

Özbek, S. (2011). *Schriften zur praktischen Philosophie am Beispiel der Türkei*. Münster: Verlag Westfälisches Dampfboot.

Pfaller-Rott, M., et al. (Eds.). (2018). *Soziale Vielfalt: Internationale Spziale Arbeit aus interkultureller und dekolonialer Perspektive*. Springer: Wiesbaden.

Quintero, P., & Garbe, S. (2013). *Kolonialität der Macht. De/Koloniale Konflikte zwischen Theorie und Praxis*. Münster: Unrast.

Rehklau, C., & Lutz, R. (2007). Internationale Themen. In L. Wagner & R. Lutz (Eds.), *Internationale Perspektiven Sozialer Arbeit*. Wiesbaden: VS Verlag.

Saal, B. (2013). *Kultur, Tradition, Moderne im Spiegel postkolonialer Differenzbewegungen: Eine interkulturelle Kritik der Moderne*. Mainz: Wissenschaftsverlag.

Spivak, G. C. (1999). A critique of postcolonial reason. New York, London.

van Bimsbergen, W. (2002). *Ubuntu* and the globalisation of Southern African thought and society. https://www.quest-journal.net/shikanda/general/ubuntu.htm

Tlostanova, M. V., & Mignolo, W. D. (2012). *Learning to unlearn – decolonial reflections from Eurasia and the Americas*. Columbus: The Ohio State University Press.

Vazquez, R. (2012). Towards a decolonial critique of modernity. BuenVivir, relationality and the task of listening. In R. Fornet-Betancourt (Ed.), *Capital, poverty, development. Denktraditionen im Dialog: Studien zur Befreiung und Interkulturalität* (pp. 241–252). Aachen, Mainz: Wissenschaftsverlag.

There Are Many Roads to a School of Social Work. Importance of the International for Modern Social Work

Rebekka Ehret

Abstract

The aim of this chapter is to explore the histories of four academic schools of social work. Their common denominator is the circumstantial and influential force of armed conflicts and war. Their stories of origin are set apart by time and socio-political space. The two cases of the Global North (Berkeley, US; and Lucerne, Switzerland) are connected to World War I, the two cases of the Global South (Sulaimani, Iraq; and Freetown, Sierra Leone) are embedded in a post-civil war context. While the first two cases are shaped by the national, the others are shaped by the international in relation to problem and target group definition, which contributes to a post-indigenization paradox. As a result, professionalizing social work as an intervention is also seen as a method to sensitize the public to society's social problems.

Keywords

International social work • Schools of social work • History of social work • Global south • Global north

R. Ehret (✉)
Hochschule Luzern Soziale Arbeit, Luzern, Switzerland
E-Mail: rebekka.ehret@hslu.ch

1 International Social Work: History and Associations

International social work is gaining ground in the debates about social work and its history, topics, theories, methodologies and positions. Contributions to international social work range from field practice to transnational research, from lecturer and student exchanges to postcolonial critique, from intercultural perspectives to historical analyses. International social work covers aspects of research as well as practice. Topics include poverty, gender, health, religious fundamentalism, armed conflict, migration, development, community care and individual case management across borders (Wagner and Lutz 2018).

In the definition of social work by the International Federation of Social Workers (IFSW), it is maintained that professional social work promotes social change, helps to solve problems in social relations, as well as empowering and liberating human beings. As a profession, it uses theories to explain social behaviour in the context of social structures, and mediates in a theoretically informed way between individuals and their social environment. The profession is guided by the principles of human rights and social justice (IFSW Europe i. V. 2010).

Having attended the final conference of the DAAD cooperation project between the Protestant University of Applied Sciences in Bochum (Germany) and the University of Sulaimani (Kurdistan-Iraq) in October 2019, and consequently becoming more interested and involved in the establishment of schools of social work in the Global South, I redirected my focus toward Sierra Leone. Like Kurdistan-Iraq, Sierra Leone has been heavily affected by armed conflicts and civil wars. In both countries, the establishment of a school of social work is closely connected to the sufferings induced by armed conflicts and the wish to assist those who have suffered the most in an informed manner. In her opening speech, Professor Cinur Ghaderi made this fact clear when she said to the international audience: 'Social work in Kurdistan does not take place in a vacuum. It is contextualized in the structure of society and embedded in cultural traditions, modern transformations and a space affected by permanent injustice, war, violence, and experience of suffering' (Ghaderi and Sonnenberg 2021, p. 15). It was that very space, engendered by the experience of a decade-long civil war, which caused the two university colleges of Sierra Leone, Njala in Bo and Fourah Bay in Freetown, to establish a school of social work in the respective departments of Sociology.

The crucial initiating role of wars and armed conflicts caused me to seek a better understanding of the historical context in which my own school of social work (University of Applied Sciences and Arts in Lucerne, Switzerland) and the School of Social Welfare at Berkeley (University of California), where I had spent my sabbatical in 2017, were founded. As will become clear below, in both of these cases, it was World War I and its socio-economic consequences that had a direct influence on the establishment of the two schools. However, while the two cases of the Global North during the early twentieth century are embedded in two growing national welfare states providing social security, the two cases in the Global South are situated in the context of a rudimentary social security system, where informal and non-governmental forms of social security systems prevail while, at the same time, international pressure grows.

Taking into account the above-mentioned issues, concerns and problems of international social work, a discussion of the four cases provides an interesting insight into the debate on international social work. The guiding question runs as follows: How can the establishment of social work as an academic discipline in the Global South as well as in the Global North be critically discussed when considering the nation-based social security system embedded in the welfare state on the one hand, and the growing international pressure through global social policy action and the international community on the other?

2   A Colorblind Need for Professionalization

The difference in the settings of the four cases with regard to time and space provides an interesting ground on which the need for professionalization can be discussed. There is evidence that social reformist movements came to North America from England and Germany through immigrants who continued their projects, which were informed by philanthropic ideals. Their endeavors can be subsumed under the title *Charitable Organizational Societies* and the movements of the *Settlement Houses* (Schmocker 2019, p. 2). The overall goal was to reduce poverty among immigrants in a geographical space, and in an era characterized by industrialization, protestant ethics and individualism. It can therefore be said that the birth of social work is a project embedded in colonialism and colonial modernity. In our pursuit of a critical view on international social work, we must therefore be aware of the limits of population representation and knowledge production. The important phase between 1909 and 1923, during which the debates about theory and definitions of social work were conducted by Mary Richmond (Charity Organizations) and Jane Addams (Settlement House), fell in a time when methods of conceptualizing the 'other', that is, the poor, were framed in colonial terms. The reforms display many merits, such as turning alms—defined by what people achieved—into services that were defined by what people needed (Charity Organizations), and programs to reduce structural poverty (Settlement Movements).

Yet the processes always entailed a reorganization of structures that ignored its colonial and colorblind character (Miller 2018).

When looking at one of the founding mothers, Jane Addams, it is remarkable how she, as a liberal anti-racist activist and reformist, devoted her life to the struggles for women's suffrage, immigrant education, health care, children's rights, peace and progressive education (Schugurensky quoted in Healy 2014, p. 738). She also helped to found important human rights organizations, such as the National Association for the Advancement of Colored People (NAACP). Yet, apart from this specific example, in all of Addams's fights against poverty and deprivation, it was the white poor and deprived that became the default standard for all poor and deprived in the US. This argument is sustained by the fact that there is a large body of literature which shows how, at the time, immigrants were turned into 'whites', that is they were assimilated into the white Anglo-Saxon culture of the US. With reference to Rivka Shpak Lissak, Miller (2018) maintains that the whole Settlement House Movement as well as the Hull House functioned as an important support of this process of assimilation into whiteness (p. 46). It was by becoming 'white' that upward social mobility became a possibility.

Looking at Addams's *Democracy and Social Ethics,* where she pleads with the privileged classes to help the less privileged and where she addresses the female population in particular as 'the modern woman' (p. 85), it is by default the *white* modern woman that she addresses. Maintaining her universalist ideals that equal rights should apply to anybody regardless of race, gender, class or ethnicity, she cautions the settlement workers to not over-differentiate, but to unify the residents ('solidarity of the human race'). Jane Addams hence not only advocated ignoring racial differences in the fight against class differences, but she also ignored her own whiteness. By doing so, she kept (re-)producing white supremacy and settler colonialism on the path to professionalizing social work. Miller (2018) concludes that '(…) through Addams's writing, we see that whiteness, as understood through the social evolutionary framework, was *the* idea for which they worked' (p. 64).

What impact does this implicit supremacy of white settler colonialism, exemplified in the figure of Jane Addams, have on the processes of professionalizing social work in academic institutions? And how, on a more general level, can we discuss social work as a profession working along and with boundaries? To what extent are bound representations in terms of, for example, gender, race and class being (re)produced? What does it imply for young social workers to be trained in the Global South, where they themselves are somehow affected by the phenomena that cause them to study social work? What does it mean to be privileged, to actually work as a social worker instead of being worked with?

3 Disciplinization of Knowledge in Social Work Then and Now

We saw that the gradual coming into existence of a professionalization of social work was linked to the training of mostly middle-class women, who, in the US, were usually white. Professional training for women was also one of the results of the women's liberation movement at the time, and the field of charitable work was an adequate entry into the professional world.

However, in a wider context, professionalization was linked to the—albeit slow—birth of the welfare state in the industrialized Global North. Material poverty of working-class people in the era of industrial capitalism towards the end of the nineteenth century increased, to which the gradually emerging political response was a national social policy system. Therefore, the category of the poor as the target group for social policy measures to be administered by trained social workers is a concept that came into being alongside industrialization, urbanization and the labor movement. Obviously, poverty existed before that, but the task of taking care of deprived people was assigned to members of the extended families, the church or other charitable organizations. The political pressure caused by masses of dispossessed laborers who depended on finding work and being able to work, and hence got organized in labor unions to articulate their political demands and claims for social security, ignited the (partial) shift from privately organized support in case of need to a system of financial support, administered by the public sector.

As we shall see, with the first two case studies, the growing welfare state defined other categories of people who needed support, such as orphans, the elderly, widows, sick or handicapped people, or underemployed and otherwise healthy people. Along with the foundation of the national welfare state, the need to produce knowledge from and for various types of social institutions (Matter 2011, p. 14) grew. In addition, this knowledge needed to be systematized and codified, or, in other words, disciplined in order to be successfully taught to future administrators of public resources.

Switzerland and Lucerne
Alongside Zurich and Geneva, the training institution for social fields in Lucerne was among the first ever to be established in Switzerland. At the beginning of the twentieth century, the institution in Zurich, the Soziale Frauenschule, was modelled after the above-mentioned Settlement Movement, whereas the institution in Geneva, L'Ecole des Etudes Sociales pour Femmes, and the one in Lucerne— which developed from the Swiss Catholic Women's Association—were designed

after the Alice Salomon School in Berlin. All three schools were founded in the spirit of progressive women's liberalization ethics; yet, at the time, they were also not uninclined towards Fascist ideas.

Historical analysis of their welfare work shows that, after the introduction of state custodianship in 1908, eugenicist ideas of the then-prevalent medical-psychiatric discourse were applied when, for example, female guardians were sterilized or when what was seen as a 'loose way of life' was a good enough reason to place somebody, mostly women, under guardianship (Hauss 2002, p. 106). Even though the writings of Alice Salomon were compulsory reading at the two German-speaking schools, when Salomon asked for asylum in Switzerland in 1937, her request was not granted, and nobody from the Swiss schools seemed to put in a word for her. Moreover, the rhetoric of the women in charge of the schools reminds us overwhelmingly of the then-prevalent German nationalistic discourse (ibid., p. 109).

Social (care) work and its professionalization in Switzerland is a gendered, middle-class answer to the obviously difficult living conditions of workers and their children. Members of the middle classes were shocked and appalled by the consequences of poverty that could be seen not only in housing conditions, but also in hygiene- and health-related issues. This promoted the wish to help, yet members of the middle classes were also afraid of social unrest within the working classes. This promoted the wish for control. With the implicit use of social evolutionary thinking, the middle-classes placed themselves above those they tried to help.

In contrast to Zurich, which belongs to the liberal Protestant part of Switzerland, Lucerne belongs to the more conservative Catholic part. Therefore, the Catholic Church organized the teaching of social work in the latter region. In 1918, the Swiss Catholic Women's Association developed a teaching program for women, mainly for those from wealthier and educated backgrounds, to carry out volunteer work amongst poor people to prevent social unrest and restore social order in the sense of a conservative Catholic women's movement. This was no coincidence, as the First World War brought deprivation and poverty, even to the politically neutral country of Switzerland. The most prominent articulation of social unrest was the Swiss general strike of 1918. Women trained in social and charitable work were perceived as motherly home-providing actors participating in efforts of appeasing the 'unleashed' laborers (Schmocker 2018, p. 257).

One of the most famous women who graduated from the school was Clara Reust, who, after getting her degree in 1944, worked for the NGO Pro Juventute and was co-responsible for their significant project 'Children of the Country Streets', which was carried out between 1926 and 1973. The focus of the project was the assimilation of the itinerant Yenish people in Switzerland achieved by forcibly removing children from their parents and placing them in orphanages or foster homes as a source of cheap labor.[1] About 590 children were affected by the program. This so-called 're-education' had the goal of forcing Yenish families, and particularly the whole next generation, into a 'sedentary' lifestyle (Galle 2016).

It was only in the early 1950s that the definition of social work from a Catholic perspective was replaced by an orientation toward disciplines like sociology, psychology, philosophy, law and economics, and—from 1960 on—men were allowed to become trained social workers as well. Hence, the school was renamed School for Social Work. The cultural revolution of the late 1960s and 1970s has left its traces in the curriculum of the School of Social Work, as it is now informed by the basic principles of empowerment and partiality as well as by awareness of the paradoxes of professional practice within the given political and legal framework. Specifically, Staub-Bernasconi (2007, 2016), who defines Social Work as a human rights profession based on empirical research, has had a significant impact on developing its status as a University of Applied Sciences and Arts.

Berkeley and the USA
In the case of Berkeley, the establishment of the School of Social Welfare goes back to a graduate program in Social Welfare that was started in the Department of Economics in the middle of the First World War (1917). The founder was Jessica Blanche Peixotto, the second female student at the University of California at Berkeley who was awarded a PhD and later became the first woman to hold a professorial title. Her dissertation was a comparative study of the French Revolution and modern French Socialism. Peixotto gained her academic title in 1900 under the supervision of the founder of the Department of Political Science. In 1904, she was appointed lecturer in sociology and as such taught courses on Contemporary Socialism. Due to academic differences with the head of Sociology, she joined the Economics Department as an assistant professor in 1912, where she set up the foundation for the theory of social economy, which in turn served as the foundation of the School for Social Welfare in 1944 (Burawoy and Van Antwerpen 2001; Edleson 2020).[2]

---

[1] The Yenish people describe themselves as a not fully sedentary community that has lived in Switzerland (and other European countries) for centuries. Since 2016, the Yenish (as well as the Sinti) have been recognized as a national minority in Switzerland (Berset 2016).
[2] I am very grateful to Professor Jeff Edleson, UC Berkeley, who is presently writing a biography of Jessica Blanche Peixotto and who provided me with very valuable information during my stay at UC Berkeley in February/March 2020.

Given the information in her lectures, it is safe to assume that she preferred economics to sociology, for sociology as practiced at Berkeley did not meet with the scientific standards she thought were necessary to promote change (the head of the department did not have a PhD) (Dzuback 2006). She insisted on empirical research in order to develop and implement evidence-based social policies. She taught the students of the program that it was necessary to evaluate the effect of poverty on families and children through meticulous empirical research. She also saw the need for trained social workers who would act as advocates for proper wages once they knew about the effects of poverty. In her lecture on *Control of Poverty* (1923/24), she mentioned, among many other aspects, that students must know the distinction between standards of living and the actual income of people in order to assess poverty. She also insisted that students should know to what extent this distinction had increased in significance since the end of the First World War to articulate their informed professional opinion on the minimum wage legislation (pp. 26–28). In order to understand the causes of poverty, as she stated repeatedly in her lecture, 'more facts and clearer thinking' (p. 42) were needed. By 'facts' she meant individual case studies in the field which students should undertake, as well as more sound statistical data that was needed in order 'to shift emphasis from sentiments to facts' (Peixotto 1923, p. 60).

Overall, the effects of the Great War substantially influenced and shaped her endeavors to establish a university course for training professional social workers. US participation in the war triggered a shift towards more government involvement in social assistance and a push towards more state control over private charitable organizations. One of the groups of people that were targeted to receive state support were the war veterans and in particular widows and children. The poverty induced by industrialized capitalism, on the other hand, was still something that private charitable organizations had to deal with (Grell and Lammert 2013, p. 79). Peixotto, however, did not make that distinction. She hoped that the emerging methods of social sciences could be used to bear on the well-being of poor workers, families and children, whether the cause was that the parents could not earn an income because they were veterans or because they did not have a job. She was especially concerned about poor children. She served on several statewide and national child welfare boards and spoke frequently on social well-being, using data she gathered in her studies. She gave a whole lecture on '*the child and the state*' (Edleson 2020, p. 11). Like Addams, Peixotto was interested in the sources of structural poverty, but unlike the Chicago model for Social Work, she was interested in academic research, in theory and in developing social policies and interventions based on evidence. She was not a political activist.

In addition to the study of social economics, students of social welfare also had to do field work with the Associated Charities of San Francisco. Peixotto initiated the fieldwork training during the war with a program for the Red Cross and home service workers. The American Association of the Schools of Social Work accredited her curriculum in 1928, seven years before her retirement.

Later on, after the independent School of Social Welfare had been established (1944), the civil rights movement and the women's and disability rights movements of the 1960s and 1970s contributed greatly to the development of the department and the recognition of the school's importance.

Slemani and the Kurdish Region of Iraq
In the case of Slemani, the establishment of the Department of Social Work at the University of Sulaimani happened almost one hundred years later, in 2015. At that point, it started to offer students academic training to become professional social workers. The establishment of the graduate program is tightly linked to the history of armed conflicts in the region. Ghaderi and Saleh Karim (2019) have shown how Kurdistan has witnessed many wars and seen many humanitarian crises over the last decades, but has now turned into a 'safe haven for refugees' (p. 163). Comparable to other regions on the globe, people in flight seek to remain near their homes and try to take refuge, either as internally displaced people (IDP) within their own country or as refugees in neighbouring countries (UNHCR Global Trends 2015). The US invasion and the armed conflict followed by the war against the Islamic State caused a migration pattern which has resulted in the fact that about a third of the population in Kurdistan are refugees and the overall population has increased by 30% in just a few years (Ghaderi and Saleh Karim 2019, p. 164). Within the refugee group, there is a high diversity ranging from Iraqis as internally displaced people, to Kurdish and Arab refugees from Syria, to Yazidis and Christians taking refuge from the ISIS and Arab-Sunni families (ibid., p. 169; Savelsberg 2017, p. 63).

The Kurdish region of Iraq is interesting because, since 2003, it has been constitutionally semi-autonomous, which means it has executive, legislative and judicial powers (Worldbank 2015, p. 13). It has its own military defense body and regulates its own economic and external policies as well as border and visa control, all independent of the Iraqi state government. Since 2003, it has been receiving 17% of Iraqi oil revenues and, due to its stability, it has remained attractive for foreign investors (Savelsberg 2017, pp. 62–63). Since economic and security conditions have improved, the poverty level is relatively low, with 4.5% compared to 20.5% in the rest of Iraq (https://sustainabledevelopment.un.org/hlpf/2019#vnrs).

The two favorable conditions are, firstly, transition to economic growth and progress, not least because of newly found gas and oilfields, and, secondly, the labor force, not least because of the influx of IDP and refugees.

The government has granted residency permits to the refugees, which include the right to work, free access to education and health services, and freedom of movement within the Kurdish state. Refugees without residency permits receive education and health services in the refugee camps (Ghaderi and Saleh Karim 2019, p. 172). In addition to that, the government has also developed a social protection program that includes social insurance (a pension system for the public sector and a social security scheme for the private sector) and various labor programs including a lending system for small enterprises as well as training and employment support (Worldbank 2015, p. 83). Nonetheless, the need for trained social workers to participate in relief programs is substantial. The most pressing needs are connected to the most vulnerable groups, like refugees with mental health problems, victims of torture and sexual violence and people with physical disabilities (Ghaderi and Saleh Karim 2019, p. 174).

This context is important for understanding the establishment of the Department of Social Work since it is embedded not so much in a nation-based social security system, but a region-based development that lends its particular characteristics. Due to the political history of the region, there is a strong local sense of solidarity promoting informal cooperative and reciprocal support in the community which might at times be also connected to ethnic interests. Moreover, there is a strong civil society, often organized along lines of topical interests of (inter)national NGOs that engage in violence and conflict related issues.

When looking at the establishment of social work in Slemani, the high profile of these NGOs and their articulated need for professional social workers becomes apparent in three aspects. Firstly, during the process of institution building, relevant NGOs participate in the definition of, for example, social problems, target groups for intervention and fields of research. Secondly, they facilitate the transfer of knowledge between the university and civil society, and, thirdly, they contribute to the inherent international and hence transcultural nature of training and research. This aspect is intensified by the fact that the Department of Social Work at the Bochum University of Applied Sciences has been a partner institution organizing various conferences, research, and exchange programs.

Freetown in Sierra Leone
In the case of Sierra Leone (a former British colony and protectorate), the civil war that lasted from 1991 to 2001 was followed by Disarmament, Demobilization and Reintegration (DDR), the establishment of an international criminal court,

namely the Special Court for Sierra Leone (SCSL), and a Truth and Reconciliation Commission (TRC). These institutions were introduced from outside the country and brought with them (among other things) the concept of professional social workers and social work as a profession. However, before this substantial international intervention, social care workers and voluntary organizations engaging in social care work had already existed; they were usually laypeople and trained by churches, mosques, UN bodies or by various NGOs.[3]

From within, the experience of a decade-long civil war caused the two university colleges of Sierra Leone, Njalain Bo and Fourah Bay in Freetown, to establish a School of Social Work in the respective Departments of Sociology. As one of the students of social work at Njala told me, his professor decided that citizens needed a fuller understanding of the connections between poverty and deprivation and the origins of the war. At Njala, the Bachelor's Degree program in Social Work became operational in 2009, the program at Fourah Bay College followed in 2016. The professor is said to have called it 'the forgotten half of the solution for our social problems,' thus stressing the idea that theoretical knowledge of sociology needed to be geared towards its practical application.[4]

What happened during the time between the end of the war in 2001 and the present is historically significant. During this time, the two university programs were implemented. When the war ended, Sierra Leone was seeking to attain middle-class status by 2015, but the outbreak of Ebola in 2014 caused a dramatic setback. Post-conflict attributes that Sierra Leone had been combating, such as a high level of youth unemployment, corruption and weak governance, returned and worsened due to the Ebola outbreak. Real income per capita, estimated at US$ 469.80 in 2018, is among the lowest in the world and remains well below the pre-Ebola level of US$ 562.80. Thus, in spite of its abundant natural resources and mainly young population of almost eight million people, Sierra Leone is still one of the poorest countries in the world and continues to face the challenge of enhancing transparency in managing its natural resources and creating fiscal space for development. The country is among the largest producers of mineral resources, such as iron ore, diamonds, titanium, bauxite and gold. There has been a slow but continuous decrease in poverty, but at least 50% of the population still live below the poverty line, that is, to have an income below US$ 1.90 per day. There is a substantial discrepancy between urban and rural areas. The poor in rural areas rely

---

[3] Unfortunately, there are hardly any published references to be found. One exception is the paper by Mriand J. T. Kamara that documents the activities of social care workers for the year 1970/71 (Kamara 2010). In an oral communication, a former employee of CARE International told me that there had been social care workers since 1964.

[4] Personal communication by one of his students.

on subsistence farming, and show physical isolation and lower rates of education because of poor infrastructure. Urban areas, on the other hand, face high rates of migration, accompanied by corresponding social problems (Kiendrebeogo and Mansaray 2019).

The need for a strengthened social work profession and hence for adequate professional training has become clear as social problems are challenging the country and the welfare infrastructure. Alongside the general problem of poverty, other social problems need to be addressed, like drug use, needs of people with HIV/AIDS and persons with disabilities—particularly amputee victims of the war—and persons with mental health issues, especially those traumatized during and in the aftermath of the war. Moreover, most pressingly—as in every armed, conflict-ridden country—women and girls are most vulnerable to gender-based violence and are therefore in need of special protection measures developed by professionals[5].

During my visits to Sierra Leone in 2019 and 2020, I learned about the challenges in developing social work as a profession. There is only a limited number of faculties, and as most come from other disciplines, only very few have social work practice and teaching experience. Most lecturers seem to have had more exposure to theory than direct involvement in social work practice. I also learned that there are severe shortages of culturally appropriate curricula and educational materials in general. There is no access to the internet for faculty members. However, the social workers can register with the National Association of Social Workers (SLASOW), which was founded in 2015 and became a member of the IFSW in 2017.[6]

4 Discussion

We have seen that in the cases of all four countries, the direct or indirect personal experiences of armed conflict, the economic consequences of wars, the political changes brought forth by the subsequent interventions and peace-building processes, as well as the socio-cultural responses concerning moral responsibility, play a role in establishing social work as an academic discipline. In its nature as an academic discipline, it is an educational product brought forth from Western societal

---

[5] I am very grateful to Dr. Abdul S. Kamara, Fourah Bay College, who provided me with very valuable information during my stay in Freetown in December 2019.

[6] To what extent SLASOW has a leading role in developing a national social work and social welfare policy is open to further research.

structures, ideas and values that conform to the concept of professionalism. Yet at the same time, in each case, the focus of social work knowledge seems contingent on the historical and local situation, and the product is interpreted within the local frame of reference, because it addresses context specific problems.

According to Füssenhäuser, social work as a profession relates to problems, challenges and settings in the realities of the social world and is concerned with its local effectiveness, whereas social work as an academic discipline is remote and free from the need to implement any type of action in the field. It is therefore permitted to reflexively analyse the actual situation and design possible alternative measures (2011, p. 1648). As a discipline, it targets truth and trueness. Knowledge acquired at an academic institution of social work differs from taken-for-granted knowledge (cf. Berger and Luckmann 1967), insofar as it allows the social worker to advise the clients about reasons in a decision-making process that they cannot see or think of at a given moment in time or in a given situation (Dewe and Otto 2011, p. 1132). The professional social worker's knowledge is informed by social work theory and empirical research.

Another aspect of professionalization is the development of a professional code of ethics which contributes to the recognition of the work as a profession, differentiated from other, overlapping professions. Professionalization can be seen as a process of demarcation and negotiation of boundaries. We can observe this process in all four cases at various stages. On the one hand, social work as a profession engages in negotiating its own boundaries. And, on the other hand, it negotiates the role of social workers as professionals. While the profession develops through the disciplinization of academic knowledge and the teaching of that knowledge, social workers as professionals develop their specific competencies. Invariably, both of these processes happen in the given political, economic, legal, social and cultural context within a specific local frame of reference, one on a macro- and the other on a micro-level.

There is, however, a contextual difference between the two cases from the Global North and the two scenarios from the Global South, which I call the post-indigenization paradox. When we look at Lucerne and Berkeley, where the nation state and the development of the welfare state is embedded in a national context, professionalization went very much hand in hand with the development of national institutions and organizations. Examples would be: social security schemes with their administrative body, national umbrella NPOs and NGOs bringing various smaller interest groups together—like Pro Juventute for Switzerland, and the Children's Year Committee for California—or schools and homes for specific groups of people with specific needs. The demarcation processes and the boundary negotiations mentioned above were significantly shaped by the idea of *the national*. In contrast, when we look at Slemani and Freetown, these processes and negotiations are shaped by what is happening on the *transnational* and *international* levels. In these cases, professionalization is contingent with developments within transnational civil society, the institutions of international criminal justice and other international organizations like the United Nations High Commissioner for Refugees (UNHCR). Here, the international community is turning into a global organization apparatus that produces transnational network structures with a focus on social work problems.

The difference between these two routes to professionalization is crucial because it affects questions of definition. What exactly is the problem that is observed and defined as a problem, and when does professionalizing social work seem to be the answer? How is this problem represented? How are the different players and groups differentially affected by the type of representation? What inequities and inequalities exist concerning the problem? How can the intervention 'professionalizing social work' be organized to improve the situation? How can we assess whether inequities and inequalities have been reduced or even reproduced by the innovation?[7] In the cases of the Global North, educated middle-class women saw poverty among the national population as a problem. Poverty resulted in issues such as inadequate childcare, hunger, dense housing and social unrest, at a time when industrial capitalism was expanding. Charity organizations and capital existed, as well as a moral feeling of responsibility towards deprived people. However, critical observers like Peixotto, the Catholic Women's Association and others noted that assistance was not distributed in a transparent way and was connected to exercising power over deprived people. Therefore, in their minds, professional social workers could solve part of that problem. On top of that, if social work was taught in an academic institution, sound empirical data could be collected on the basis of which welfare policies could be designed. The problem is presented as a group differential, divided by social class. No differentiation is made by race, ethnicity, nationality or sexuality, but by fields intersecting with gender, such as veterans, single mothers, men who needed a motherly guideline and age, that is, children and youths. These middle-class women did not have any first-hand experience of the war, yet they saw the effects of the war, on people, on the economy, on families and on the welfare system.

For the cases of the Global South, we have much less knowledge. Professionalization of social work as well as the processes of establishing social work in academia is hardly recorded. For Slemani, the contributions in this book are the first comprehensive publications since Ghaderi and Saleh Karim (2019), Harding

---

[7] The questions are adapted from Hankivsky et al. (2014).

and Libal (2012) and Dünnebacke (2019). For Sierra Leone, there is no literature available (yet) to inform us about the state of social work and its professionalization in academia. There are news reports and blogs about social work programs at Fourah Bay College, Milton Magai College and Njala University, and about the association Social Work Sierra Leone, which is the leading organization for social workers and acts as a pressure group. However, to my mind, other factors are also relevant. Based on my own observations and personal communications in Slemani, as well as in Freetown, additional driving forces behind the establishment of social work as a profession are people who have either been educated abroad and come back, or are still living abroad while maintaining transnational relationships with the academic institutions and colleagues in said countries. Something crucial regarding the process of problem definition is happening here. Whereas the problems of the groups defined as vulnerable are a direct result of civil wars and armed conflicts (such as amputees, refugees, domestic violence victims, etc.), an increase in social problems in general (for example, school dropouts, sexual violence, teenage pregnancy, drug abuse) plays a significant role. In the context of the Global South, emphasis is placed on the need for raising and building awareness. Therefore, professionalizing social work as an intervention is also seen as a method to sensitize the public about society's social problems. From the limited information available, one might argue that, in these cases, developing academic knowledge is tightly connected to political action. Also, in this context, due to the overwhelming presence of international organizations, a degree in social work might be one of the few entry tickets to this particular job market.

5   Demarcations of the Roads to a School of Social Work

The selection of the four cases is subjective. They are four cases I have been exposed to, that I have become familiar with and that have piqued my interest on a multitude of levels. Their common denominator is the embeddedness in war and armed conflict. They span over a time of roughly one hundred years and they raise crucial questions about the international aspect of international social work. In academic institutions of social work in countries of the Global North, the interest in international social work is one among many other interests and foci. They have emerged within nation-based social security systems embedded in the welfare state. Academic institutions of social work in the Global South, however, are inherently international. They are informed by a way of thinking that is shaped by global social policy action and discourses in the international community. In that respect, they have become de-territorialized. Yet, at the same time, they provide a negotiation platform for ideas and notions of and about social work because they are informed by local knowledge and experience as well.

If international social work is to be taken seriously today and in the future, we must learn much more about the everyday life experiences of those locally involved in promoting and supporting social work. We must also know more about the structural and historical circumstances in their countries, and the *liminal* nature of providing social services. It is sometimes simply a matter of chance whether one is the provider of social services or the provided for when both have suffered from the ravages of war.

References

Berger, P., & Luckmann, T. (1967). *The social construction of reality. A treatise in the sociology of knowledge*. New York: Anchor Books.

Berset, A. (15 September 2016). Jenische und Sinti bereichern die Schweiz. https://www.admin.ch/gov/de/start/dokumentation/medienmitteilun-gen.msg-id-63783.html.

Burawoy, M., & Van Antwerpen, J. (2001). Berkeley Sociology: Past, Present and Future. November. https://burawoy.berkeley.edu/PS/Berkeley%20Sociology.pdf. Accessed 18. May 2011.

Dewe, B., & Otto, H.-U. (2011). Profession. In H.-U. Otto & H. Thiersch (Eds.), *Handbuch Soziale Arbeit: Grundlagen der Sozialarbeit und Sozialpädagogik* (pp. 1131–1142). München: Reinhardt.

Dünnebacke, L.M. (2019). *Soziale Arbeit in Kurdistan-Irak und Deutschland – ein Vergleich am Beispiel von Genderstrukturen. Empirische Zugänge im internationalen Dialog. Genderstudies – Interdisziplinäre Schriftreihe zur Geschlechterforschung* (Bd. 32). Hamburg: Dr. Kovac.

Dzuback, M. A. (2006). Berkeley Women Economists, Public Policy, and Civic Sensibility. Women, Gender & Sexuality Studies Research. 40. https://openscholarship.wustl.edu/wgss/40.

Edleson, J. L. (2020). Jessica Blanche Peixotto and the Founding of Berkeley Social Welfare (Revised May 29, 2020). https://drive.google.com/file/d/1Z8XrTiIeqLDeYBSmk53MLgRFEeikFDDu/view.

Füssenhäuser, C. (2011). Theoriekonstruktion und Positionen der Sozialen Arbeit. In H.-U. Otto & H. Thiersch (Eds.), *Handbuch Soziale Arbeit* (pp. 1646–1660). München: Reinhardt.

Galle, S. (2016). Kindswegnahmen: Das „Hilfswerk für die Kinder der Landstrasse" der Stiftung Pro Juventute im Kontext der schweizerischen Jugendfürsorge. Chronos.

Ghaderi, C., & Saleh Karim, L. (2019). Social work with refugees in Kurdistan Region in Iraq. In M. Pfaller-Rott, A. Kállay, & D. Böhler (ed.), Social Work with Refugees. European Research Institut for Social Work (ERIS) Monographs Volume V, pp. 163–184.

Ghaderi, C., Sonnenberg, K. (2021). Framing the Topic – a Multi-Dimensional Approach to Social Work in Post-War and Political Conflict Areas. In Sonnenberg, K., Ghaderi, C. (Eds.), *Social Work in Post-War and Political Conflict Areas.* (pp. 1–25) Wiesbaden: VS

Grell, B., & Lammert, C. (2013). *Sozialpolitik in den USA, Eine Einführung.* Wiesbaden: Springer VS Verlag.

Hankivsky, et al. (2014). An intersectionality-based policy analysis framework: Critical reflections on a methodology for advancing equity. *International Journal for Equity in Health, 2014*(13), 119.

Harding, S., & Libal, K. (2012). Iraqi refugees and the humanitarian costs of the Iraq war: What role for social work? *International Journal of Social Welfare, 21,* 1.

Hauss, G. (2002). The Locations of Women in the History of Social Work: Three Examples from German-Speaking Switzerland, In H. Sabine & W. Berteke (Eds.), *History of Social Work in Europe (1900–1960). Female Pioneers and their Influence on the Development of International Social Work Organisations.* (p. 105–119.) Opladen: Leske and Budrich.

Healy, K. (2014). *Social work theories in context: Creating frameworks for practice.* Houndmills: Macmillan International Higher Education.

IFSW Europe. (2010). *Standards in social work practice meeting human rights.* Berlin.

Kamara, Mriand J. T. (2010). *Case studies from Sierra Leone (AG3303-2-1-2). Association for Social Work Education in Africa (ASWEA) Papers, 1971–1989.* Johannesburg: ASWEA

Kiendrebeogo, Y., & Mansaray, K. (2019). *Sierra Leone – Economic diversification study (English).* Washington, D.C.: World Bank Group. https://documents.worldbank.org/curated/en/354291578288053592/Sierra-Leone-Economic-Diversification-Study.

Matter, S. (2011). *Der Armut auf den Leib rücken. Die Professionalisierung der Sozialen Arbeit in der Schweiz (1900–1960).* Dissertation. Zürich: Chronos.

Miller, L. (2018). *Critical whiteness studies and American pragmatism in dialogue: A Jane Addams case study.* Doctoral dissertation, University of Colorado at Denver.

Peixotto, J. B. (1923). *Econ 180: The control of poverty.* Berkeley: University of California Press.

Savelsberg, U. E. (2017). 10. Irakisch-Kurdistan zwischen Flüchtlingskrise, sinkenden Ölpreisen. FACT FINDING MISSION REPORT.

Schmocker, B. (2018). 100 Jahre Ausbildung in Sozialer Arbeit in Luzern: Meilensteine. In G.-S. Pia & S. Beat (Eds.), *Soziale Arbeit bewegt, stützt, begleitet* (pp. 255–281). transcript: Luzern.

Schmocker, B. (2019). Die internationale Definition der Sozialen Arbeit und ihre Sicht auf Profession und Sicht der Sozialen Arbeit. https://avenirsocial.ch/wp-content/uploads/2018/12/Die-IFSW-Definition-und-ihre-Sicht-auf-die-Soziale-Arbeit-1.pdf.

Staub-Bernasconi, S. (2007). Vom beruflichen Doppel- zum professionellen Tripelmandat. Wissenschaft und Menschenrechte als Begründungsbasis der Profession Soziale Arbeit. https://www.avenirsocial.ch/de/p42006222.html.

Staub-Bernasconi, S. (2016). Social work and human rights – Linking two traditions of human rights in social work. *Journal of Human Rights and Social Work, 1*(1), 40–49.

UNHCR Global Trends (2015). Forced Displacement in 2015. "The UN Refugee Agency, UNHCR, 2015." https://www.unhcr.org/statistics/unhcrstats/576408cd7/unhcr-global-trends-2015.html.

Wagner, L., & Lutz, R. (2018). Internationale Soziale Arbeit zwischen Kolonialismus und Befreiung. Eine Einleitung. In L. Wagner, R. Lutz, C. Rehklau, & F. Ross (Eds.), *Handbuch internationale soziale Arbeit. Dimensionen – Konflikte – Positionen* (pp. 7–21). Weinheim: Beltz Juventa.

World Bank (2015). *Kurdistan Region of Iraq: Economic and Social Impact Assessment of the Syrian Conflict and the ISIS Crises*. World Bank, Washington, DC.

Systematising Local Knowledge: Hierarchies, Power Relations and Decontextualisation in West–East Knowledge Transfer

Karin Mlodoch

Abstract

Based on the author's long-standing research and work experience in the realm of psychosocial counselling for women survivors of violence in the Kurdistan Region of Iraq, the paper reflects on the current influx of mostly Western-shaped concepts of trauma, psychosocial and social work into the region. It takes a critical look at the hierarchies and colonial aspects inherent to the West–East knowledge transfer and its tendencies towards de-contextualisation and marginalisation of local knowledge and practices. Drawing on examples of local practices in trauma care and psychosocial work, it presents approaches of systematising local practices and knowledge of social work, and takes a critical stance towards the construction of a dichotomy between local and global knowledge and the risk of 'culturalising' different approaches to social work. It thus contributes to the debate on the development of participative and equal platforms and mechanisms of knowledge transfer, theory–practice transfer and knowledge exchange in the realm of international (psycho)social work.

Keywords

International social work • Knowledge production • International knowledge exchange • Mental health and psychosocial services (MHPSS) • Trauma • Psychosocial trauma • Kurdistan region of Iraq

K. Mlodoch (✉)
HAUKARI – Association for International Cooperation, Berlin, Germany
E-Mail: mlodoch@haukari.de

1   What is Knowledge?

Knowledge is still widely perceived as something objective, something valid independent of subjective perceptions, and largely associated with claims of truth. Such an understanding of knowledge finds its sharpest form in the neoliberal concept of a 'knowledge society', which sees scientific knowledge as a key tool of human control over nature, economic innovation, and increased productivity. Progress optimism is inherent to this normative concept as well as the definition of 'development' from a capitalist perspective and the related diagnosis of 'development deficits' in less industrialised countries.[1] The current worldwide crisis due to the spread of the Covid-19 virus in 2020 sheds light on the global priority given to evidence-based disciplines and at the same time on its limits when it comes to questions of ethics and (global) social justice.

Ever since the 1960s, such normative understanding of knowledge has been questioned and criticised by social anthropologists and by post-structuralist and post-colonial thinkers. They question the related claims of objectivity and truth, pointing instead at multiple 'knowledge systems' and the embeddedness of knowledge in historical, social, economic, and cultural contexts and focus on understanding *'knowledge production processes'*. They further criticise the reductionist view of knowledge as scientific knowledge, which disregards other forms of knowledge based on customs, experience, body, and emotions and have introduced the term *knowledge practices* which underlines the process nature of knowledge. The Norwegian social anthropologist Fredrik Barth (2002, p.1, quoted from AutorInnenkollektiv 2010, p. 8) has defined knowledge as 'what a person employs to interpret and act on the world'.[2] His perception of knowledge includes not only information but also emotions, skills/capacities and language and underlines the embeddedness of knowledge in social relations. Anthony Giddens (1984) defines knowledge as agency. And Michel Foucault (1975) has shown the close interrelation between knowledge and power in his landmark opus 'Discipline and Punish'.

Moreover, multiple studies of cultural anthropology, ethnology and postcolonial studies have criticised the dominance of Western concepts of knowledge, which are shaped by the European enlightenment period and rationalist individualism and marginalise and devaluate other non-Western forms of knowledge

---

[1]For a detailed description and critique of the concept see the paper 'Wissen und Soziale Ordnung – Knowledge and Social Order' by a research group at the Humboldt University Berlin, (AutorInnenkollektiv 2010).

[2]Interestingly Frederik Barth travelled to the Kurdistan Region in the 1950s and has done research and publication on the social organisation of the Kurdish society (Barth 1953).

(e.g. Said, 1979). The Indian feminist Gayatri Chakravorty Spivak (1988), one of the main thinkers of postcolonial theories, criticises Eurocentric concepts of knowledge and stresses that knowledge is never innocent but always driven by power interest. Against the background of colonial history, she points at the institutional and structural obstacles inhibiting the colonised and subaltern from speaking, takes a radical stance against Western patronising through knowledge-export, and defines Eurocentric knowledge as a tool of further colonisation and thus 'epistemic violence' (Spivak 1988, p. 70).

This paper refers to an understanding of knowledge as produced and shaped by socio-economic and political contexts, as embedded in, and a result of, social relations and practice and driven by various interests and power relations. By looking at the example of the psychological concepts of *trauma* and *resilience*, the paper will show how knowledge travels and transforms in the West–East knowledge transfer and discuss hierarchies, ambivalences, and interests in this transfer.

2 Example of Travelling Knowledge – the MHPSS (Mental Health and Psychosocial Services) Focus in International Aid and Development Cooperation and the Concepts of Trauma and Resilience

Trauma and *resilience* are two concepts developed within psychological research and practice in working with victims and survivors of violence, war and disasters. In their historical development, both concepts have had a strong emancipatory connotation in making visible the psychological scars of war and violence. The work and research with Holocaust survivors (e.g. Bettelheim 1943; Keilson 1979; Laub 1992), victims of Latin American dictatorships (Martín-Baró 1990; Becker 1992), and women and children who are survivors of gender-based and sexual violence (Herman 1992) has largely contributed to the development of the concept of trauma and its understanding as an overwhelming individual and social experience of shock and violence, which destroys the physical and psychological integrity of the victims as well as their self- and world-assumptions and confidence. It was the political movement of US-Vietnam veterans which ultimately successfully lobbied for the introduction of psychological trauma as a clinical syndrome in international health manuals. Its classification under the term 'post-traumatic stress-disorder' (PTSD) marked the recognition of the psychological impact of violence and gave impetus to survivors to claim for pensions and reparations, and to bring perpetrators to justice.[3]

Ever since, multiple concepts of trauma and tools of trauma care have developed – sometimes contrasting, sometimes enriching each other – and controversies have emerged between differing approaches and therapies. Greatly simplifying, there are on the one hand clinical approaches, such as the PTSD-concept or concepts from cognitive, behaviourist and neurobiological schools, which translate into individual and symptom-centred trauma therapies, often focusing on exposure to the traumatic event and/or on behavioural and cognitive changes. On the other hand, there are approaches informed by psychoanalytic and systemic frameworks, which underline trauma as a not purely individual but also social experience as well as the political and socio-economic embeddedness and process character of trauma, and advocate for integrated approaches of psychological support with activities for stabilising life conditions and empowerment. Within these controversies, the concept of resilience has had an important role and emancipatory connotation in shifting the focus from deficit- and symptom-oriented perspectives on trauma victims to the survivors' resources, strengths, agency and empowerment (e.g. Boss 2006).

Currently, against the background of multiple protracted wars and conflicts around the world and some 70,8 million of refugees worldwide,[4] the concepts of trauma and resilience have gained increasing attention in the realm of international humanitarian aid and development cooperation. Under the terminological umbrella of 'MHPSS – Mental Health and Psychosocial Support', international governments, organisations and donors have increased their investment and engagement in the sector of psychosocial support for survivors of violence and war. The German Federal Ministry of Economic Cooperation and Development engages with UNICEF and other international organisations for 'scaling up and increasing long-term structural MHPSS interventions in protracted and post-conflict settings' (UNICEF & BMZ 2018, title and pages 17–25).[5] At an international conference in Amsterdam 2019 international donors, policymakers,

---

[3] For an overview on the historical development of the trauma concept and the main approaches and controversies in the trauma field see Mlodoch (2017).

[4] United Nations High Commissioner for Refugees (2020). Figures at a Glance. 19.6.2020. https://www.unhcr.org/figures-at-a-glance.html

[5] UNICEF and BMZ: REBUILDING LIVES. Addressing Needs, Scaling Up and Increasing Long-term Structural MHPSS Interventions in Protracted and Post-Conflict Settings. REPORT Expert Meeting Berlin 4–5 July 2018. Available at:https://www.unicef.de/blob/190 328/783fd057e51a7e971fa0186ce037052d/report-rebuilding-lives-expert-meeting-berlin-4-5-july-2018-data.pdf. Title and pages 17–21.

humanitarian aid specialists and MHPSS practitioners came together under the slogan 'Mind the Mind Now' and advocated for making MHPSS a standard component of humanitarian aid (Ministry of Foreign Trade and Cooperation Development, The Netherlands 2019). Such platforms have great merit for putting the psychological impact of violence on the political agenda and urging decision makers and donors to consult with researchers and practitioners for policy and funding decisions.

Undoubtedly, the increasing focus on MHPSS is of great importance to countless survivors of terror, war, conflict and sexualised violence throughout the world. Often, trauma centres are the only safe places for them to refer to for speaking out on their suffering. This is especially true for women, for example the group of Yazidi women in Iraq, who have been enslaved, raped and humiliated by the terror militia ISIS for months and years, and for whom stigmatisation by their own communities adds to their suffering.

At the same time, there are also problematic aspects. First, when looking through the MHPSS-lens at regions of conflict and war, there is a tendency to diagnose whole populations as 'traumatised' and in need of psychological support, a perspective which individualises, pathologises and once again victimises survivors of violence. More generally, the MHPSS-focus bears the risk of deviating attention from the political and economic sources of war and conflict and thus de-contextualise and de-politicise the impact of war and violence.

With no pending political solutions for most of the current conflicts in the Middle East and worldwide, the increasing MHPSS focus is also largely driven by European governments' security interests and containment policies to strengthen 'resilience' of communities affected by war and conflict and keep them from fleeing their home regions. Indeed, *resilience* has become a central category in national and international humanitarian funding policies and has replaced previous foci such as sustainable development (Merk 2017). Within this framework, the concepts of trauma and resilience are stripped of their political and emancipatory dimensions and co-opted as tools for making people 'Fit For the Disaster' (booktitle from medico international 2017). At an international conference on 'The Politics of Trauma and Resilience' in Germany in 2018,[6] psychosocial practitioners from 16 European, Middle Eastern, African and Latin American countries illustrated their dilemma of offering trauma care in the midst of ongoing war situations despite their knowledge of the central role that safety and stability play

---

[6]The Conference was organised by medico international, HAUKARI e.V., BAfF e.V. and Fatra e.V. and brought together practitioners from international humanitarian aid and development and the work with refugees in Europe.

for such care. They also criticised that in the midst of situations of crisis and displacement, they do have access to funding for psychosocial activities, while there is a lack of support for covering people's basic economic needs and the strengthening of sustainable services. Pauline Boss, a pioneer of resilience research, warned:

> 'We have to be careful not to adopt a model of resilience, that consolidates the status quo. (…) We cannot accept war and poverty as a permanent condition as if nothing could be done against it. We cannot accept that the individual's resilience is the only response. Individual health is a core criterion for resilience, but we have to address that people can only grow in a healthy society and environment' (Boss 2006, p. 85).

3 Which Knowledge? – The Example of Western Transfer of Trauma and Psychosocial Knowledge in the Kurdistan Region of Iraq

In 2014, the terror militia ISIS advanced into large parts of Syria and Iraq. The massacres and atrocities ISIS committed, including the devastating enslavement of thousands of women from the Yazidi community, left a trail of death, destruction, suffering and displacement among individuals and communities throughout the region. At the peak of the crisis in 2016, Iraq counted 3.4 million Internally Displaced People (IDPs)[7]; 1.5 million of them were hosted in the Kurdistan Region of Iraq. Here, the ISIS-related conflicts added to multiple layers of previous episodes of war and violence during the Iran-Iraq war and Saddam Hussein's Baath-regime in the 1980s, two US-led invasions in 1991 and 2003 and multiple internal political and sectarian conflicts.

Ever since the advance of ISIS, Iraq and the Kurdistan Region of Iraq have seen a substantial influx of humanitarian aid, mostly addressing internally displaced persons, refugees and victims of ISIS-related violence[8] and with a specific focus on psychosocial support and trauma care. With increased funding of MHPSS-activities, numerous international and local NGOs have set up trauma care and psychosocial counselling centres in the Kurdistan Region of Iraq

---

[7]International Organisation of Migration (IOM). Iraq Mission (2016). Displacement in Iraq exceeds over 3.4. Million. https://iomiraq.net/article/0/displacement-iraq-exceeds-34-million-iom, accessed: 14.07.2020.

[8]Local organisations have criticised this focus for fuelling tensions between local victim groups and have promoted a more encompassing approach including host communities and victims of past violence.

and train local psychologists, social workers and governmental employees in the health and education sector in specialised trauma therapeutic approaches as well as broader psychosocial counselling skills. The German governmental development agency Deutsche Gesellschaft für Internationale Zusammenarbeit (GIZ) set up a 'Regional Programme for the Psychosocial Support of Syrian and Iraqi Refugees and Internally Displaced People' in 2015 and engaged – together with NGO partners – in the development of ethical and practical guidelines for psychosocial support and training of local professionals.[9] At the University of Duhok, an Institute of Psychotraumatology has been established in cooperation with the German University of Applied Sciences Villingen-Schwenningen and funded by German government funds,[10] offering master's studies for psychotherapists.

Generally, internationally funded MHPSS-programmes start from the assumption that there is a lack of qualified local personnel and academic expertise for implementing psychosocial support programmes and thus define an extensive need of training local professionals. While there is indeed only a small number of trained psychologists and psychotherapists in the Kurdistan Region of Iraq, and Departments of Social Work at local universities have been established only recently, this assumption tends to overlook the rich experience and expertise in dealing with violence and suffering in local government health and social services as well as in numerous civil society organisations, humanitarian initiatives and human and women's rights organisations – expertise gained from decades of constant conflict and crisis in the region. It also overlooks the rich variety of local strategies developed by local communities in coping with trauma and crisis beyond professional contexts.

Consequently, within the MHPSS-programmes, there is an increase in the abundance and variety of training opportunities, most of them designed for academics and professionals in the psychosocial sector and involving international external educators. The range of concepts and methods transferred within these trainings is wide and differs according to the respective methodological and conceptual approaches of implementing NGOs and educators: from trauma-sensitive holistic psychosocial approaches to largely Western-shaped individual PTSD-approaches or short-term neurobiologically informed exposure therapies like Narrative Exposure Therapy (NET). The adaptation of the latter to unsafe und unstable contexts of ongoing crisis has been severely questioned from both professional and ethical perspectives and is subject to controversial debates among

---

[9] See: GIZ – Psychosocial Support for Syrian/Iraqi Refugees and Internally Displaced People, https://www.giz.de/en/worldwide/39799.html (retrieved 15.04.2020).

[10] See https://web.uod.ac/ac/institutes-and-centers/ipp-institute/

psychosocial researchers and practitioners (see e.g. Mundt, Wünsche, Heinz & Pross 2011; Ottomeyer 2011a, 2011b).

Trainees report that international educators often lack knowledge of the local context and are not informed about the complex situations local practitioners work in: the cases of overlapping political, social and gender-based violence they are dealing with, as well as their own stress and burdens. Often, they themselves have gone through traumatic experiences, share the precarious life situations of their clients and are harassed and stigmatised during their work when interfering in clients' social, psychological and family issues. Thus, educators often fail to address the concrete challenges faced by trainees in their work or set standards which are not applicable to the specific work situation. Requests for individual settings granting privacy to the client might be difficult to meet in overcrowded IDP camps or in situations with strong family control, where clients might prefer to have another family member as a witness at their side. Attempts to limit their role to that of a confided psychosocial counsellor might have to be abandoned when local practitioners must act as psychosocial and legal counsellors at the same time and involve police and judiciary with clients in life threatening situations (author's observations; see also Meintjes et al. 2019).

Trainees furthermore report on duplicated trainings, and trainings with often conflicting content and information. They are left puzzled by differing 'technical' information, for example regarding the question if a client fulfils a PTSD-diagnosis after three months or rather six months of continuing grief after the traumatic event, but also by more fundamentally differing approaches, e.g. whether to encourage survivors of violence to speak out on their experience, or rather bolster resilience and coping in order to avoid the risk of re-traumatisation by exposure to the traumatic event (ibid.).

The trainees' consternation points towards a more general problem: Rarely do educators outline the psychological school or conceptual framework they refer to, the underlying assumptions to the approach and methods they teach, possible controversies related to their approach and potential alternative approaches. Doing this would enable trainees to understand the whole picture and choose the methods they consider helpful for their own contexts. Thus, the complexity and historical and political dimension of trauma concepts, the controversies within the trauma debate and the variety of different approaches arrive in bits and pieces in the Kurdistan Region of Iraq. Local colleagues are confronted with numerous methods and tools of trauma work, each one presented as the one and only, with confusing and disempowering effects.

To summarise, a double de-contextualisation occurs in the West–East-transfer of trauma concepts: a lack of contextualisation to the local conditions and a de-contextualisation of the very trauma concept itself. Furthermore, there is still a prevalence of Western-shaped scientific approaches to trauma in training for local professionals and thus a tendency to overwrite and marginalise local knowledge and practices, and specifically overlook local strategies of coping with trauma and working with survivors which are not explicitly articulated in a formal education sector.

The following two examples from the Kurdistan Region of Iraq shall illustrate what is meant here by local knowledge: the collective ways of coping with trauma developed by women Anfal survivors and the women-centred family mediation strategies developed by local women groups working with survivors of gender-based violence.

4 Local Practices, Example 1: Local Strategies in Dealing with Mass Violence and Trauma – Women Anfal Survivors in the Germian Region[11]

In 1988, the Iraqi Baath-regime conducted a vast military operation against the Kurdish region, deporting and killing more than one hundred thousand men and women and destroying thousands of Kurdish villages. Survivors were held in detention for months, beaten up, humiliated, and witnessed the death of numerous older people and children from hunger and exhaustion. After their release, they were forcibly resettled in camps, so-called 'collective towns', where they remained even after the Kurdistan Region gained provisional autonomy in the aftermath of the first US-led invasion in Iraq in 1991. For another 15 years, the survivors lived in uncertainty about the fate of their deported relatives and in precarious economic situations without support from the government or international organisations. For the women among them, most of whom had lost husbands, and often many other male relatives, social marginalisation added to economic constraints. Within a patriarchal and traditional rural environment, their legal and social status as women without men was unclear; they had to defend the honour of their missing male relatives without their protection and provision. They did different

---

[11] The paragraph is based on the author's work and long-term psychological research with a group of women Anfal survivors in Rizgary and the Anfal Women Memorial Forum Project. Notes on the women's situation during and after Anfal, their coping strategies and subjective perceptions derive from in-depth interviews with women Anfal survivors in the Germian region between 1999 and 2011 (Mlodoch 2014).

kinds of hard labour to survive and feed their children, yet were exposed to social control and stigmatisation when doing so. They were constantly torn between the struggle for survival on the one hand, and, on the other hand, dominating gender patterns expecting them to be mourning women.

Against these constraints, the women survived. Their most powerful resources, they say, were their children, who gave them hope and energy, and the strong collective networks they developed: they helped each other with daily challenges, went out to work jointly, defended each other against social stigmatisation and jointly raised their children. They developed a specific way of speaking about their experience during Anfal and in the aftermath, interweaving their own stories with those of other women into one collective and shared Anfal narrative. In the midst of adverse existential conditions, this collective way of narrating Anfal made it possible for them to speak out and at the same time gain protection within the group from overly painful exposure to their individual traumatic memories. Thus, they found a specific way of dealing with what Judith Herman (1992) describes as the central dilemma of trauma: the wish to speak out on the one hand, and the desire to silence the experience on the other.

Women Anfal survivors' situation did not change until 2003, when the Iraqi Baath-regime was overthrown and the sanctioning of the Kurdish region as an autonomous region in a federal Iraq brought about a sense of safety and political stability. At the same time, they gained painful certainty regarding the death of their missing relatives. The main perpetrators were brought to justice and executed, giving a sense of justice to Anfal survivors. The Kurdistan Regional Government gave pensions and housing to Anfal survivors, thus stabilising their economic situation. With increased certainty and economic stabilisation, women Anfal survivors reconstructed their families and social and economic networks together with their grown-up children. They are still in grief and suffer from a range of symptoms which might qualify for a clinical PTSD-diagnosis, such as nightmares, waves of pain, anxieties and depression. But they firmly reject defining their suffering in psychological terms. They consider their nightmares as normal reactions to the abnormal experience they had.[12] Moreover, they reject the idea of healing associated with trauma care offers as a betrayal of the dead and of their own identity as Anfal survivors, which brings both stigma and distinction. Indeed, approaching the women with individual trauma-therapies would not

---

[12] In his report about survival in the Nazi concentration camps the Austrian psychiatrist and Holocaust survivor Viktor Frankl stated, that 'in an abnormal situation, abnormal reaction is a normal behaviour' (Frankl 1982, p. 30).

only fail to meet their articulated needs, but also individualise them and thereby undermine their consoling and empowering collective structures.

Today, feelings of satisfaction and pride of having survived and brought up their children without societal and male support exist alongside their sense of suffering and they strongly and collectively articulate their claims towards the Kurdistan Regional Government, the Iraqi government and the international community for justice, compensation and political acknowledgment, as well as for memory sites to honour victims and survivors.

In the town of Rizgary in the Germian area in the South of the Kurdistan Region, a group of some hundred women Anfal survivors have been campaigning for a self-designed and self-administered memory site to represent their specific suffering as well as their strengths during and after Anfal. The site is designed to be a place of remembrance as well as a social forum for them to maintain their collective structure and jointly advocate for political acknowledgement. For more than ten years, they have been meeting with local and international architects and artists, as well as Bosnian and Rwandan survivors of genocide, and they have visited Holocaust memorials in Germany to discuss the design of the memorial. They have successfully campaigned to be assigned a construction site for the memorial and a budget from the Kurdistan Regional Government. Through the project, they have been strengthening their collective structures and created multiple spaces for jointly processing their individual and collectively shared memories. They have significantly contributed to challenging the dominant national Kurdish discourse on Anfal, which depicts women survivors as passive mourning victims, and instead established a counter-narrative of strong women. They have also brought their claims into the public debate. Thus, the project combines psychosocial and even therapeutic aspects with empowerment and the strengthening of survivors' self-organisation structures.[13]

---

[13] The Women Anfal Survivors Memorial Forum Project has been supported by the German NGO HAUKARI since 2009 with funds from the German Federal Foreign Office. For more information see: www.haukari.de

5 Local Practices, Example 2: Family Mediation Strategies in Psychosocial Work with Women Survivors of Gender-Based Violence[14]

Gender-based violence is widespread in the Kurdistan Region of Iraq, including the killing of women and men due to pre- or extra-marital relations or disobedience to their male relatives. Women accused of adultery and prostitution face imprisonment. More recently, the widespread abuse of social media has added new forms of violence as men harass women or discredit their reputation when women do not give in to their advances.

Since the late 1990s, women and human rights organisations in the Kurdistan Region of Iraq have addressed the issue of gender-based violence and successfully campaigned for legal reforms, such as the amendments to the *Iraqi Personal Status Law* which were passed for the Kurdistan Region in 2009 and strengthen the rights of women in marriage, divorce, and child custody. In 2011, the Kurdistan Regional Parliament passed Act No. 8 of *Combating Domestic Violence in the Kurdistan Region of Iraq*, which sanctions physical and psychological violence including female genital mutilation and the exclusion from education with terms of imprisonment. The Kurdistan Regional government has set up governmental shelters for women and established the General Directorate of Combating Violence against Women (DCVAW) under the umbrella of the Interior Ministry. The DCVAW runs hotlines, referral points and counselling centres with civil and police staff, which combine psychosocial and legal counselling on the one hand with protection for women affected by violence by investigating and pursuing perpetrators on the other hand. These achievements are under constant attack from traditional and religious structures and have seen a roll-back with the recent ISIS-related crisis and the strengthening of militarist, nationalist and fundamentalist discourses.

Local women organisations such as the Social and Cultural Centre for Women KHANZAD in Slemani closely cooperate with governmental institutions; women who flee their families and seek support are often in life-threatening situations, so that close cooperation with police, judiciary and governmental shelters is essential for protecting them. Moreover, the dominant concept of family honour and shame does not consider independent life perspectives for women outside the family

---

[14]This chapter is based on the author's longstanding cooperation and work relation with the Social and Cultural Center for Women KHANZAD in Sulaimani, Kurdistan region of Iraq, as well as other women organisations and NGOs engaged in protection and counselling for women in situations of crisis and violence. See also Mlodoch (2019).

context, and social control is too tight to allow women to live with alternative identities anonymously out of reach of their families. In addition, the family context is the mainstay of social relations, the central source of a sense of belonging, emotional support and the reference system of identity. Consequently, most of the counselling processes focus on family and community counselling and mediation as central strategies for women's counselling projects like KHANZAD as well as in governmental DCVAW-counselling centres.

In the counselling process, priority is given to the woman's safety, e.g. by referring her to a government refuge in a life-threatening situation. Counsellors will outline different legal options, from denouncing perpetrators to more reconciliatory approaches of family reunion, and encourage the woman to take her own decision regarding the aim of the counselling process. If she opts for legal measures, she will be accompanied by the KHANZAD team throughout all judiciary steps. However, in most cases, the counselling team engages in intense family mediation processes, often over several months, together with or on behalf of the concerned woman with both her father's and her husband's family. Through family mappings they identify potentially supportive family members and engage them, as well as external moderators such as teachers, religious leaders or local politicians in the locations concerned. In confronting the perpetrators, they use a combination of threatening them with legal sanctions on the one hand and offering conciliatory approaches on the other hand, thereby negotiating solutions step by step. Solutions might be, for example, the reconciliation of wife and husband under the condition of continuous follow-ups; or a father's family consent to the daughter's divorce with guarantees of reintegrating her into the family.

Local psychosocial counsellors have developed rich and sophisticated tools and skills in accompanying women through such mediation processes and often reach solutions even in highly escalated situations which involve the threat of honour killings, by convincing the harassers to renounce the killing of their daughters or wives and sign such a renouncement at Court. The mechanism at work here is that at the very moment when the DCVAW or the KHANZAD counselling team – often accompanied by a lawyer or even police – enter in negotiations including family and external stakeholders such as local authorities and religious leaders, the private family issue is brought into a semi-public sphere. This intervention opens a door for fathers/brothers threatening to kill their daughters/sisters when they themselves are under pressure by their peer group to restore their 'honour'. It gives them a way to refrain from the murder without losing face by pointing to political interests, possible damage to their region or legal sanctions involved. Once they refrain from the honour killing decision, the door is also open for a conciliatory solution and, in some cases, even for the return of the respective woman into her family and the restoration of family ties.

These mediation processes build upon community reconciliation processes inherent to the local context but have been further developed into a women-centred psychosocial counselling tool. However, local counsellors are well aware that family reunion is not always the best choice for the women's individual perspectives. Indeed, there is intense reflection among the counsellors involved on the tendencies of such family approaches to consolidate repressive family systems. Therefore, besides individual counselling, both governmental offices and civil society organisations are engaged in awareness raising and educational activities, in campaigns for women's economic independence and free choice of partners, and in political advocacy against gender-based violence and for gender equality.

6 Institutional and Social Barriers to Local Practices

Both of the examples described above illustrate local practices of dealing with the impact of political and social violence in the Kurdistan Region of Iraq. In the first example, they have been developed by survivors of violence themselves. In the second example, they have been advanced by practitioners from local women's organisations and counselling projects, many of whom have come to psychosocial practice through women and human rights activism rather than through formal education as psychologists or social workers.

Consequently, such practices rarely find their way into formal training offered in trauma care and psychosocial counselling under the MHPSS umbrella. They are instead overlooked and marginalised due to language and access barriers, particularly in training designed for academically educated local professionals from medicine, psychology, social work and social sciences. Such barriers are reinforced by the local Kurdish political and academic elites, among them an increasing number of MHPSS-experts with access to international funding, exchange and travel. For the educational policy of the Kurdistan Regional Government, alignment with Western academic discourses and knowledge is of high importance and associated with concepts of progress and modernisation on the one hand, and of connectedness and protection of Kurdish autonomy rights in times of crisis on the other hand. Recently, there have been controversial debates in the Kurdistan Region on government plans to introduce English as the main language in university teaching of Humanities and Social Sciences. This move would certainly accelerate access to international academic debates, but at the same time create new structural barriers for students from remote contexts in accessing university education, undermine the development of contextualized Kurdish research and practices and further deepen the often criticised gap between theory and practice in academic education.

In 2016, HAUKARI and the German-Kurdish psychologist Cinur Ghaderi brought together practitioners from women counselling projects in the Kurdistan Region, most of them without formal professional education. Following the concept of 'systematising local knowledge' the training's intention was to encourage participants to gather their daily practices and case studies, relate them to broader psychological and methodological frameworks and document them in order to establish links with broader and academic debates on psychosocial work. While the meetings were described as an empowering experience by most participants, the envisaged documentation did not materialise, partly due to the lack of time and writing experience of the local colleagues, but also due to their internalised perception that their 'stories' would not qualify for academic writing.

Endeavours to create platforms of mutual knowledge exchange are challenged to not only ask 'which knowledge' but also 'who can speak?', and to tackle institutional and social barriers against integrating local practices from non-formal sectors, which are hitherto unheard and underrepresented in academic and professional debates.

7 The Dichotomy of International/Global and Local/Indigenous Knowledge

Within the critical discourse on the hegemony and colonial aspects of Western knowledge and its claim for universalism, much attention has been given more recently to notions of local knowledge, traditional knowledge or indigenous knowledge in social sciences. These notions refer to knowledge developed in countries of the Global South and/or in colonised and oppressed communities. In 2014, the International Federation of Social Work has integrated the notion of indigenous knowledge into their global definition of social work, thus including reflections on the influence of post-colonial theories and giving credit to post-colonial thinking.[15]

While the importance of this shift from Western universalism to the consideration of alternative forms of knowledge is undisputed, the often made-up, artificial

---

[15] International Federation of Social Work (2014). Global definition of social work. Available at: https://www.ifsw.org/what-is-social-work/global-definition-of-social-work/

dichotomy between global and local, between Western and indigenous knowledge, brings its own problems.

First, there is an underlying assumption about the existence of 'cultural boxes', of closed knowledge systems, which is to be questioned in a globalised world with constant migration of people, concepts and knowledge.

Furthermore, there is a tendency of blurring the terminological distinction between local, traditional and indigenous knowledge. Local knowledge is largely considered to be related to traditions, cultural patterns, customs and local beliefs. Thus, the hierarchy between Western 'scientific' knowledge on the one hand, and local, 'traditional' knowledge on the other hand is perpetuated, once again othering local expertise instead of looking for similarities across contexts.

More recently, European psychologists and social workers working in refugee and migrant contexts increasingly refer to Middle Eastern colleagues in order to learn from their expertise in dealing with extended families, frameworks of 'honour and shame' and phenomena such as forced marriages. This is an example of mutual learning; yet this exchange also focuses on the local colleagues' very specific knowledge of dealing with extended families in Islamic shaped contexts. This means that such knowledge is removed from the broader socio-economic contexts (Lanzano 2013) in community and family focused societies and from the colleagues' broader theoretical frameworks. Their experience is thus 'culturalised'.

Indeed, the above described examples of local practices in dealing with trauma and violence have little to do with culture or tradition, but rather with historical and political context, socio-economic conditions and dominant gender patterns. Women Anfal survivors have developed collective strategies and memory practices in response to shared experiences of mass violence, socio-economic constraints and disempowering gender roles and victim discourses. Local women's organisations have gathered rich and sophisticated expertise in women-centred family mediation strategies in a patriarchal environment marked by women's socio-economic dependencies on their families.

The South African psychologist Berenice Meintjes is engaged in training and exchange with local practitioners in the Kurdistan Region of Iraq. Based on her work for the South African NGO Sinani – Kwa Zulu Natal Programme for Survivors of Violence,[16] which gives psychosocial support to conflict-ridden communities in the Kwa Zulu Natal province, she presents Sinani's approaches and practices of the Kurdish colleagues in this volume. The Sinani team had found clinical and individual approaches to trauma insufficient for addressing the needs in

---

[16] See www.survivors.org.za

communities marked by a constant cycle of political, social, economic and gender-based violence and developed community-based approaches instead, including a controversially discussed partnership proposed by tribal elders for implementing traditional cleansing ceremonies as collective reconciliation practice. Some of the Kurdish colleagues working with women affected by gender-based violence rejected the idea of integrating traditional elders and ceremonies into psychosocial practice, stating that this would consolidate the very structures they try to leave behind and weaken their struggle against gender-based violence. An intense exchange developed during this – as it could be defined – South-South-exchange among South African and Kurdish colleagues on the differing contexts and their shared dilemma between constructively using locally inherent traditional structures and family systems on the one hand, and their commitment to social change and emancipatory practices on the other hand.

The example illustrates the complex multi-directional interaction between Western concepts and locally rooted traditional practices. It also shows differing perceptions of traditional practices across contexts, both of which are dealing with powerful traditional structures. It ultimately advocates for an in-depth exchange focusing on context rather than culture.

8 Conclusion

In order to truly engage with critiques of Western dominance in knowledge transfer, a process of equal and mutual learning across contexts in the field of psychosocial knowledge and practices requires a long-term commitment instead of short-term training. Instead of merely focusing on integrating local knowledge and practices in academic and professional debates, institutional, social and language barriers in the set-up of exchange platforms have to be tackled in order to include hitherto unheard and marginalised voices, knowledge and practices from communities, survivors and non-formal working sectors. Space and time have to be given to an in-depth and multi-directional exchange on historical, political and socio-economic conditions, gender-patterns and institutional frameworks in the contexts involved. Reciprocal transparency is needed regarding the underlying assumptions and frameworks which are shaping knowledge, approaches and practices, in order to see transversal differences and similarities and enable all involved parties to make informed decisions and choices about the kind of knowledge that is helpful and useful in their own context for developing emancipatory practices of psychosocial work.

References

AutorInnenkollektiv. (2010). Wissen und soziale Ordnung. Eine Kritik der Wissensgesellschaft. Mit einem Kommentar von Stefan Beck. In: Working Papers des Sonderforschungsbereiches 640 1/2010, https://edoc.hu-berlin.de/bitstream/handle/18452/3891/1.pdf?sequence=1&isAllowed=y. Accessed 14. July 2020.

Barth, F. (1953). *Principles of social organisation in southern Kurdistan.* Oslo: Brødrene Jørgensen boktr.

Barth, F. (2002). An anthropology of knowledge. *Current Anthropology, 43*(1), 1–11.

Bettelheim, B. (1943). Individual and mass behavior in extreme situations. *Journal of Abnormal and Social Psychology, 38,* 417–452.

Becker, D. (1992). *Ohne Haß keine Versöhnung. Das Trauma der Verfolgten.* Freiburg: Kore Verlag.

Boss, P. (2006). *Loss, trauma and resilience. Therapeutic work with ambiguous loss.* New York: W.W. Norton & Co.

Foucault, M. (1977). *Discipline and Punish.* New York: Pantheon Books.

Frankl, V. (1982). *Und trotzdem Ja zum Leben sagen. Ein Psychologe erlebt das Konzentrationslager.* Munich: dtv.

Giddens, A. (1984). *The constitution of society. Outline of the theory of structuration.* Cambridge: Polity.

Herman, J. L. (1992). *Trauma and recovery.* New York: Basic Books.

Keilson, H. (1979). *Sequentielle Traumatisierung bei Kindern. Deskriptiv-klinische und quantifizierend-statische follow-up Untersuchung zum Schicksal der jüdischen Kriegswaisen in den Niederlanden.* Stuttgart: Enke.

Lanzano, C. (2013). What kind of knowledge is 'indigenous knowledge'? Transcience, a Journal of Global Studies, 4(2). https://www2.hu-berlin.de/transcience/page3_volume4_issue2.htm. Accessed 14. July 2020.

Laub, D. (1992). Bearing witness, or the vicissitudes of listening. In S. Felman & D. Laub (Eds.), *Testimony. Crises of witnessing in literature, psychoanalysis and history* (pp. 57–64). London: Routledge.

Martín-Barò, I. (1990). *Psicología social de la Guerra: trauma y terapia.* UCA editors: San Salvador.

Medico international. (2017). *Fit für die Katastrophe. Kritische Anmerkungen zum Resilienzdiskurs im aktuellen Krisenmanagement.* Gießen: Psychosozial Verlag.

Merk, U. (2017). Crisis is the new normal. Überleben in der Dauerkrise. Resilienzdiskurse in der Entwicklungszusammenarbeit und humanitären Hilfe. In (eds) medico international. Fit für die Katastrophe. Kritische Anmerkungen zum Resilienzdiskurs im aktuellen Krisenmanagement, pp. 125–151. Gießen: Psychosozial Verlag.

Meintjes, B., Grussendorf, S., Karem Saleh, L. (2019). Evaluation Report. Cooperation project HAUKARI e. V/medica mondiale. Strengthening local protection and counselling for women and girls affected by gender-based violence in IDP shelters and host communities in Kurdistan-Iraq. Available at: https://www.haukari.de/files/pdf/KRI_Evaluation_Report_short.pdf. Accessed 14. July 2020.

Ministry of Foreign Trade and Cooperation Development, The Netherlands. (2019). 'Mind the Mind Now'. Conference Special 7 & 8 October, 2019. https://www.government.

nl/ministries/ministry-of-foreign-affairs/documents/publications/2019/10/18/mind-the-mind-now-conference-special. Accessed: 14. July 2020.

Mlodoch, K. (2014). *The limits of trauma discourse. Women Anfal survivors in Kurdistan-Iraq.* Berlin: Klaus Schwarz Verlag.

Mlodoch, K. (2017). *Gewalt, Flucht – Trauma? Grundlagen und Kontroversen der psychologischen Traumaforschung.* Göttingen: Vandenhoeck & Ruprecht.

Mlodoch, K. (2019). The intersections between gender-based political, social and domestic violence – a regional exchange on psychosocial practices of supporting refugee and host community women affected by violence. Report on regional exchange meeting, May 2017, Duhok, Kurdistan-Iraq. In: The MHPSS Network. https://app.mhpss.net/?get=320/2020_03_17-report-duhok-expert-exchange-may-2017.pdf.

Mundt, A., Wünsche, P., Heinz, A., & Pross, C. (2011). Trauma therapy in crisis and disaster areas – a critical review of standardized interventions such as Narrative Exposure Therapy. *Psychiatrische Praxis, 38,* 300–305.

Ottomeyer, K. (2011). *Die Behandlung der Opfer. Über unseren Umgang mit dem Trauma der Flüchtlinge und Verfolgten.* Stuttgart: Klett-Cotta.

Ottomeyer, K. (2011b) Traumatherapie zwischen Widerstand und Anpassung. Journal für Psychologie, psychologische und therapeutische Arbeit mit Menschen zwischen Krise und Trauma, 19(3).

Said, E. W. (1979). *Orientalism.* New York: Vintage Books.

Spivak, G. C. (1988). Can the Subaltern Speak? In C. Nelson & L. Grossberg (Eds.), *Marxism and the Interpretation of Culture* (pp. 66–11). Urbana: University of Illinois Press.

UNICEF and BMZ. (2018). Rebuilding lives. Addressing Needs, Scaling Up and Increasing Long-term Structural MHPSS Interventions in Protracted and Post-Conflict Settings. Report from Expert Meeting 4–5 July 2018. https://www.unicef.de/blob/190328/783fd057e51a7e971fa0186ce037052d/report-rebuilding-lives-expert-meeting-berlin-4-5-july-2018-data.pdf. Accessed: 14. July 2020

Community-Based Psychosocial Work to Change the Cycle of Violence in Post Conflict Areas

Berenice Meintjes

Abstract

'If you have come here to help me, you are wasting your time. But if you have come because your liberation is bound up with mine, then let us work together', says Lilla Watson (The source of this quotation is credited to a speech made by Lilla Watson at the 1985 United Nations Decade for Women Conference in Nairobi). How can we collectively and meaningfully intervene to disrupt the cycle of violence which often takes place in post-conflict areas? Violence, displacement, loss of resources and the breakdown of the social fabric of family and community life often lead to ongoing cycles of violence, including revenge, displaced aggression such as domestic violence and sexual assault, early marriages, crime, corruption and extremism. Learning from community-based interventions in South Africa and Kurdistan, this paper asks provocative questions about: the model of justice that we use in our work to promote reconciliation; participatory community development; holistic support which includes economic strengthening and education; drawing on traditional and religious cleansing rituals; working with survivor support groups to address their needs; and solidarity movements for prevention of conflict, abuse, inequality and division.

This paper draws extensively on work at SINANI (www.survivors.org.za), a non-profit, non-governmental organisation (NGO) from KwaZulu-Natal, South Africa.

B. Meintjes (✉)
Jikelele Consultancy, Dargle, South Africa
E-Mail: bearpsv@iafrica.com

> **Keyword**
>
> Psycho-social • Community • Post-conflict

1 Background to the Recent Conflict

The province of KwaZulu-Natal has been a focal point for much violence for two centuries, including:

- 1787–1828: The dictator and warrior King Shaka Zulu who conquered most of the province through a series of battles with local tribes.
- 1838: Zulu-Boer war ('Boers' was the term used for Dutch immigrants)
- 1879: Anglo-Zulu war
- 1899–1902: Anglo-Boer war (during which Boers were sent to concentration camps in South Africa)

Remarkably, the previously oppressed white Boers consequently became the oppressors. During the period between 1912 and 1994, through the race classification system called Apartheid (which means separation), they divided the country by race (literally colour) groups. White South Africans gradually increased their power to take over legal power, voting power, and all government positions of power. They reserved key jobs for white people, divided the education system and secured the majority of the country's resources for a minority population. At the time, approximately 13% of the South African population were classified as 'white'.

After an extended struggle for freedom, South Africa eventually held its first ever democratic elections in 1994, and Nelson Mandela, leader of the African National Congress, became president.

2 Model of Restorative Justice

Despite many years of violent resistance, the move to democracy was eventually made with a negotiated settlement. Under the leadership of Bishop Desmond Tutu, the Truth and Reconciliation Commission was implemented. This was a legal process which included public survivor testimonies called 'hearings', which we all watched on television in South Africa. Perpetrators of violence were given amnesty if they agreed to tell the truth about what they had done within a particular time frame in the form of these public hearings—in other words: they were not prosecuted, and not imprisoned. The hearings were corroborated with the collection of evidence and multiple testimonies, and eventually published in the form of a report.

The South African Truth and Reconciliation Commission was a famous process which met with substantial international acclaim, but also with a lot of critique in studies on its advantages and disadvantages (Hamber and Kibble 1999). When I once explained this process to a group of Kurdish colleagues, they were horrified and said 'But what kind of justice is that?'. We then informally compared South Africa's attempted model of restorative justice with Iraq's model of retributive justice (led by occupying forces) in a participatory workshop with social work practitioners hosted by HAUKARI e.V. and KHANZAD Women's Centre[1] as follows (Table 1):

Table 1 Comparison of Forms of Justice

Example: South Africa	Example: Iraq
Restorative justice Truth and Reconciliation Commission: • Idea that the truth is an important aspect of healing and recovery • Concept of amnesty • Underlying concept of 'confession & forgiveness'	**Retributive justice** Public punishment of transgressions: • Punishment of leaders • Vetting of former oppressors from public service ('de-Ba'athification') • Legal punishment

While the Truth and Reconciliation Process is sometimes described as a form of restorative justice, one substantial problem with it was the lack of restitution or compensation. South Africa remains one of the most unequal societies in the world today. There have been programmes for economic transformation called 'affirmative action', which is essentially a system of employment quotas. There has also been a gradual reformation of the divided education system (which is still highly problematic and unequal). There are criticisms regarding the lack of land restitution and land reform, with a 2017 study conducted by the South African government reporting that 72% of the agricultural land is still owned by

---

[1] The workshop was facilitated as part of the project 'Strengthening local governmental and civil society structures for psychosocial counselling for women affected by gender based violence in IDP camps and host communities, Kurdistan-Iraq', funded by the German Federal Ministry of Economic Cooperation and Development (BMZ) in 2017.

white South Africans who represent 9% of the population (Rural Development Land Reform 2017). Despite recent efforts, South Africa remains one of the most economically divided countries in the world, with extreme wealth and extreme poverty (according to the World Bank Gini Index 2019).

3 Violence and the Breakdown of Social Fabric

An additional problem lies in ongoing cycles of conflict, political violence, division, domestic violence, child abuse, alcohol and drug abuse, with which—like many other countries that have experienced violent conflict—South Africa struggled. In the early days of SINANI's work, we found the model of Shaik (1994), an Indian South African, very helpful (Fig. 1):

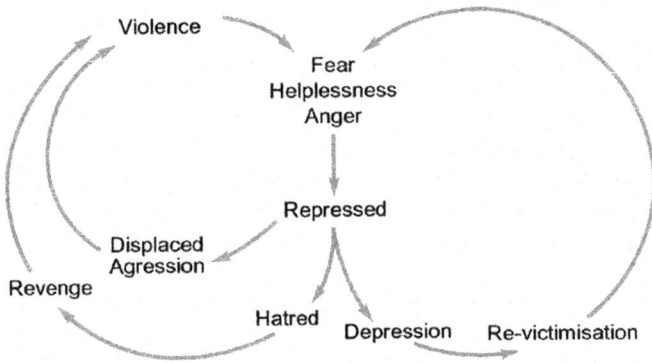

Fig. 1 Cycle of Violence Model (adapted by Meintjes 2008, originally from Shaik 1994)

4 Cycle of Violence

Coming from a psychoanalytical perspective, this model describes ongoing cycles of violence, such as:

- Revenge, which is particularly common after a perceived loss of dignity and the loss of a close family member.

- Displaced aggression, based on the psychoanalytic concept of 'Acting Out'. This can result in, for example, high rates of domestic violence and child abuse. A SINANI participant once said, 'When I remember the things that happen to me I become so angry and then I take it out on my girlfriend.'[2]
- Re-victimisation, as described in the psychoanalytic concept of repetition compulsion, where someone unconsciously exposes themselves to further harm. For example, a commercial sex worker in counselling said, 'It's like I know I am putting myself at risk, but I do it anyway. Maybe I am punishing myself for what happened to me'. A classic example would be a child who was sexually abused and then dresses provocatively to attract more sexual attention.

5   SINANI's Emerging Model of Social Work in a Conflict Area

Trauma (psychological orientation)
SINANI started with a strong psychological, psychoanalytic orientation to its work. This was followed by various models of intensive trauma counselling, with extensive training from international trauma experts. However, in real life, SINANI struggled to implement what they taught us, and lacked practical strategies that we could implement in our daily work as we continued to face significant challenges:

We often worked under extreme time constraints, and with a lack of privacy. For this, more practical support was needed. In addition, many people were still living in situations of ongoing danger. Frank Chikane (1986), in his work on the effects of violence against children living in Apartheid unrest, introduced the concept called 'continuous trauma'. The findings in our evaluation study in Kurdistan with Dr. Luqman and Dr. Kurdistan, and the students from the University of Sulaimani were similar to Chikane's proposition: that counselling cannot be separated from protection. When people are in literally life-threatening situations, the focus must lie on practical safety mechanisms first. A further problem we encountered in South Africa was that the people we were working with, experienced extreme poverty and wanted us to focus on income generation. Equally, our study in Kurdistan showed that many of the women in internally displaced persons (IDP) camps asked KHANZAD and the People's Development Organisation (PDO) to focus more on income-generating activities.

As a consequence, the following focus areas for future work were established:

---

[2]These are examples from counselling or workshops conducted by the author.

Economic strengthening
The work of Derek Summerfield (1999) was especially important for helping us to shift from intensive psychological work to social work as such, in particular with a focus on economic strengthening and practical support.

Empowerment, restoring dignity
A particularly vicious aspect of Apartheid oppression was the de-humanisation and humiliation of black South Africans. Apartheid systematically took away their dignity and made them believe that they were second class citizens—which I believe is a mechanism that is also observed in similar forms in other contexts like Kurdistan and Kosovo. Steve Biko, a South African freedom fighter and writer, put it succinctly: 'The most potent weapon in the hands of the oppressor is the mind of the oppressed.' (1972, p. 92)

Consequently, a focus of our work became 'restoring dignity', for example through the Respect Campaign where we used the concept of respect to talk about difficult issues like gender-based violence. The people in the poster images shown below, which included traditional leaders, older women, young men and women, each gave a message about treating others with respect, and how this strengthens respect between people. The selected representatives facilitated workshops in different communities, sharing their stories of how showing respect towards another person restored a damaged relationship and brought harmony and mutual respect. For example, one young male explained that when he started treating his girlfriend with more respect, their previously conflicted relationship improved. Another older woman explained that every time she passed a gang of young criminal males in the street of her village, she greeted them in a very respectful traditional manner. They were surprised and gradually started greeting her respectfully when she passed. Eventually they established a friendship and she was able to help them to explore options for furthering their education and gaining employment. Interestingly, I once shared this example in a presentation in Germany, and an older German woman who attended this presentation later told me she tried the same thing with a group of young male immigrants she passed each morning on the street in her neighbourhood. She reported the same change in their attitude towards her, such that they also established a friendly relationship (Fig. 2).

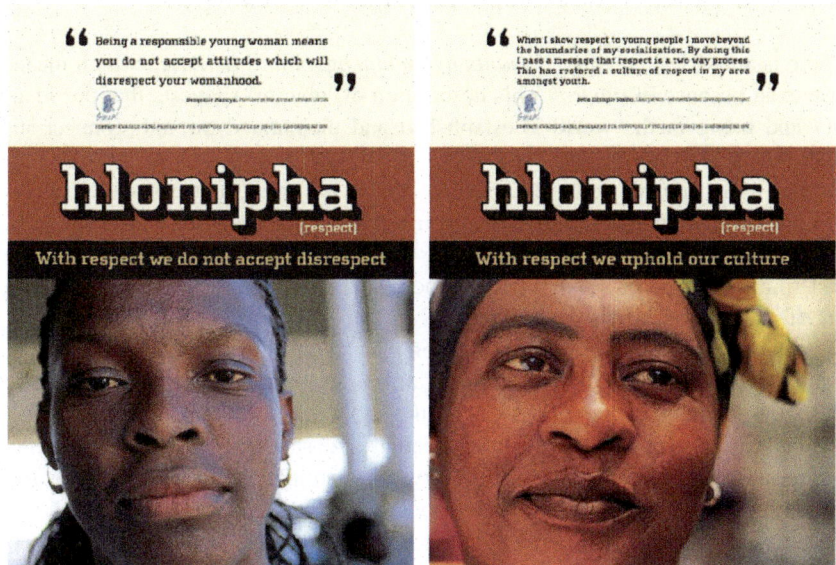

Fig. 2 Examples of two Hlonipha or respect posters produced by SINANI (2010)

Social reconnecting and empowerment
Increasingly, our work shifted towards a focus on the social dynamics involved in the conflict.

6   Fragmentation Disempowerment Model

SINANI (Higson-Smith 2003) developed a model whereby violence is not only damaging on an individual psychological level. It also breaks down the social fabric of society. It damages connections, erodes respect, and breaks down social structures which exist so that individuals can help each other. Therefore, SINANI believes that our role as social workers is more than material and economic, more than psychological. It is social, and this is why social work is such an important discipline. In Africa, we have found the concept of 'ubuntu' particularly useful to understand and frame this social dimension of our work.

7 Ubuntu—A Concept Relevant to Social Work

There is an African saying: *'Umuntu ngumuntu ngabantu' (isiZulu)*, which means 'we exist because of others'. This description of 'ubuntu' suggests that our identity and being in the world is established and maintained through connections with others.

The term 'ubuntu' thus describes a quality of connectedness which includes humanity, humanness, goodness, warmth and kindness (Gade 2011, p. 303). According to Gade (2011, p. 306), thanks to the writings of Jordan Kush Ngubane in Drum Magazine in South Africa in the 1950s, it started to be used to describe an African philosophy or worldview.

Michael Onyebuchi Eze (2008) writes that 'ubuntu' is about recognising our humanity through other people, which affirms us (builds us up). According to this view, humanity does not exist in the individual person, but is co-created through relationships with other human beings. Eze says that 'a person's humanity is dependent on the appreciation, preservation and affirmation of other person's humanity' (Eze 2008, p. 387). He proposes that we are sustained through our connections with one another, and that a person who is disconnected from others is unable to develop a full sense of self in the world.

Hence, in Africa the concept of wellbeing relies on the quality of our connections with others, both past and present, so this includes our deceased relatives. They remain as part of our psychosocial, spiritual wellbeing—and I think that we have a lot to teach Western societies about remembering the deceased, while grieving for them. Strengthening people's social connections with others builds their capacity to live a full and meaningful life.

Over time, our work shifted toward a stronger social and community-strengthening focus, based on concepts of reconnection and empowerment, and drawing on local, existing community-based traditional structures.

Cultural, traditional approaches
One day, a group of traditional leaders from a large rural area called uMbumbulu approached SINANI and said that in order to build lasting peace they needed to perform a traditional cleansing ceremony, or reconciliation ceremony. They explained that before war, warriors are traditionally given a medicine and a spiritual blessing to make them stronger, better fighters. If no cleansing ceremony is offered after the war, the men stay with this 'fighting spirit' and 'cause a lot

of trouble'.[3] SINANI found the link to Shaik's (1994, as adapted in Merk 2010) Cycle of Violence interesting.

Maybe unsurprisingly, SINANI had doubts about this idea at first. Staff were worried about the reactions of, for example, mothers who had lost a child in war might feel if they were confronted with a peace ceremony and a spiritual, ritual cleansing that allowed leaders to determine that, now, there is peace. First, SINANI asked the University of KwaZulu-Natal for a cursory study on people's reactions to this idea, especially those of women and families who had lost relatives. Similar to the study undertaken in Kurdistan with the University of Sulaimani, the lead professor, Dr Nhlanhla Mkhize (from the University of KwaZulu-Natal), used this project as an opportunity to send students into communities to do research. Secondly, SINANI asked traditional leaders to research the described cultural practise in their own communities—to consult older people in the community and research the advantages, as well as exploring the risks. Finally, SINANI was concerned about the possibility that the process might be taken over by political parties, thereby rendering the process less neutral and potentially more divisive. To avoid this, they were very careful about equality, establishing an equal panel, or task team, with representation from each political party involved. In the end, SINANI was satisfied that the ceremony would not cause further division and that the community members who had suffered extensive loss during the conflict wanted the ceremony to take place and supported the idea. Hence the ceremony went ahead and they were grateful that the King of the Zulu Nation and the leader of the KwaZulu-Natal ANC and Premier of the province came to the ceremony.

The ceremony was a large event, attended by about 10 000 people from nine local villages who had previously been in conflict with each other. Participants reported that the ceremony was very moving and had a profound impact (Körrpen et al. 2008). As part of their research, the university students talked to attendees during the ceremony, and visited them a week after the ceremony to ask about their experiences of it. Community members said that the day after the ceremony, former 'no-go' areas could be accessed by public transport again. One woman reported: 'I live next to a field where many people were killed. They used to keep me awake at night with their screaming. But the night after this event they were quiet and have not bothered me since' (Körrpen et al. 2008).

The cleansing ceremony is an example of a powerful, locally-driven process. However, this is not to say that we should support all traditional, cultural processes, as Karin Mlodoch from HAUKARI argues in her paper. Not all traditional,

---

[3] These are examples from counselling or workshops conducted by the author.

cultural and religious processes are helpful, and we should be careful not to romanticise these. This became particularly clear to me during my exchange with KHANZAD. I remember one of the KHANZAD staff saying to me, 'But we have been working for decades to get rid of some of our religious and cultural practices—why would you want to reinforce them?' In fact, a less publicised aspect of this work is that SINANI organised two more traditional cleansing ceremonies. However, as the subsequent ceremonies had not been grounded in a deep participatory, thoughtful process, they were just not as impactful. They were organised in a quicker, more superficial process, as opposed to the lengthy engagement in the first ceremony, the idea for which came from the local leadership themselves. It seemed like other communities heard about this cultural idea and wanted to replicate it. The comparison shows that this is not a recipe for social work in post-conflict communities.

Having said that, I would also argue back to KHANZAD and HAUKARI that we should not fight too hard against culture, traditions and religion. When we push too hard against a religious or cultural system, we risk reinforcing and strengthening that traditional culture. For example, a study with immigrant Indians in the Pietermaritzburg, KwaZulu-Natal (Pillay and Wassenaar 1997) looked into why these immigrant families experienced high rates of adolescent suicides. It was found that first generation Indian families were even more traditional and strict than their parents in India. This suggests that when we place a family system under too much stress, we risk pushing it towards more conservative beliefs and practices. This is often seen to be an expression of people's fear that their children will lose their cultural heritage and 'go off the rails'. And, of course, sometimes the opposite happens—too much pressure on adolescents can make them feel desperate that they have no escape (Fig. 3).

Fig. 3 Adaptation of Hart's Ladder of Participation (adapted by REPSSI 2018)

Hart's Ladder of Participation presents an alternative to suggesting that we replicate or support all traditional cultural practices, or resisting all traditional cultural practices. This model suggests that in order to truly empower people, that in order to really undo the damage of violence and oppression and humiliation, we should try to involve people meaningfully in their own development projects. This should go beyond 'tokenism' and 'decoration', enabling meaningful, self-reflective participation. Eventually, the goal is that these participants or structures lead their own social work and development processes.

Political, social & psychosocial—movement building
A fascinating aspect of working towards meaningful participation is that the work inevitably becomes more political. As survivor groups gain strength, they can develop into powerful social movements. More recently, I have had the privilege of listening to survivor groups in South Africa, Tanzania, Mozambique, Kosovo, and Kurdistan (the KHANZAD work with Anfal women).

- There is often meaningful support through solidarity structures—where local groups of people who have similar experiences and problems come together to support one another and solve problems together. Sometimes, the support that a survivor of trauma can give to another person who has been through the same experience, is more profound than psychotherapy sessions.
- When working together collectively towards legal reform, implementation of laws and upholding the government to its commitments, these social movements have great power to change society (Fig. 4).

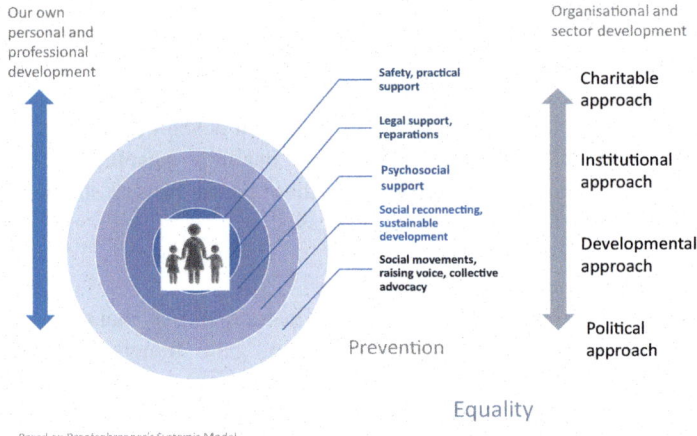

Fig. 4 Summary diagram of SINANI's development (Meintjes 2019)

The circles in the diagram above show the value of offering a holistic range of types of support, depending on the needs of the individuals, families and communities affected by conflict and adversity. This process is mirrored in our own professional development and in our approach to development, from:

- a charitable approach (where we provide practical and material support such as food and clothes);
- to a more institutional approach where we try to strengthen local structures and systems to provide assistance;
- to a more developmental approach which encourages people to reflect critically on their situation and engage meaningfully in their own developmental process;
- to a more political process in which the ultimate aim is prevention of exposure to suffering and greater equality for all.

SINANI 's journey as a South African community-based social development organisation mirrors the maturation of social work and other sectors, from a charity-based approach to institutional strengthening, and finally towards a developmental approach which involves meaningful engagement and participation. As

Ruth Seifert shows in her contribution to this volume, through these different strategies we can strive towards increasing equality, which is one of the core values that we uphold as a social work community.

Acknowledgement Thank you to HAUKARI e. V. for exchange opportunities with KHANZAD and other organisations in Kurdistan.

References

Biko, S. (1972). *I write what I like*. Johannesburg: Heinemann.
Chikane, F. (1986). Children in turmoil: The effects of unrest on township children. In S. Burman & P. Reynolds (eds.). *Growing up in a divided society* (pp. 333–345). Johannesburg: Ravan Press.
Eze, M. O. (2008). What is African communitarianism? Against consensus as a regulative ideal. *South African Journal of Philosophy., 27*(4), 386–399.
Gade, C. B. N. (2011). The historical development of the written discourses on Ubuntu. *South African Journal of Philosophy., 30*(3), 303–329.
Hamber, B., & Kibble, S. (1999). *From truth to transformation: The truth and reconciliation commission in South Africa*. Catholic Institute for International Relations Report.
Hart, R. (1970). Ladder of participation. Retrieved from: https://www.unicef-irc.org/publications/pdf/childrens_participation.pdf. Last accesses 14 Aug 2017.
Higson-Smith, C. (2003). *Supporting communities affected by violence*. London: Oxfam.
Körppen, D., Mkhize, N., & Schell-Faucon, S. (2008). Evaluation report on the Sinani peace building programme. Weltfriedensdienst (WFD), Berghof Foundation. Retrieved from: www.survivors.org.za.
Meintjes, B. (2008). Restoring dignity: Sinani handbook for trauma support workers. Sinani / KwaZulu-Natal Programme for Survivors of Violence.
Meintjes, B. (2019, unpublished paper). Community-based psychosocial work to change cycles of violence in post conflict areas. Presentation given during the International Conference: 'Social Work in Post-War and Political Conflict Areas – Challenges and Chances'.
Merk, U. (2010). Restoring dignity: Peace-building handbook. Durban: SINANI. www.survivors.org.za.
Pillay, A. L., & Wassenaar, D. (1997). Recent stressors and family satisfaction in suicidal adolescents in South Africa. *Journal of Adolescence, 20*(2), 155–162.
Regional Psychosocial Support Initiative (REPSSI) (2018). Community-based work with children and youth. module 1: Personal and professional development. Revised Edition.
Rural Development and Land Report, Republic of South Africa, Land Audit Report, November 2017.
SINANI / KwaZulu-Natal Programme for Survivors of Violence (2010). Respect Campaign Poster Series (unpublished): www.survivors.org.za.
Summerfield, D. (1999). A critique of seven assumptions behind psychological trauma programmes in war-affected areas. *Social Science & Medicine, 48*(10), 1449–1462.
World Bank Gini Index. (2019). https://data.worldbank.org/indicator/SI.POV.GINI. Last accesses 24 Sept 2020.

Children Born of Wartime Rapes – an Analysis from a Gender-Sensitive and Psychosocial Perspective

Cinur Ghaderi

Abstract

Mass rape and sexual violence continue as part of the broader strategy of conflict and war and have been documented for past and present wars. Out of these attacks, children are born. The mothers and their children—born of war—represent a worldwide, epidemiologically highly relevant group of victims in post-war countries, whose psychosocial burdens, such as social exclusion and stigmatization, as well as processing patterns and resources, have so far been neglected by psychosocial research. In this paper, the gendered dynamics of armed conflicts and political violence are reconstructed, and genocide is viewed through a gendered lens. Considering the historic, individual, and social conditions, a framework to understand the specific problems of victimized mothers and their children of rape from the scope of psychosocial sciences will be conceptualized.

Keywords

Children born of war • Psychosocial aspects • Conflict-related gender-based sexual violence • Transgenerational traumatization • Political violence

---

Talk given on Monday, 21st October 2019 at the International Conference: Social Work in post-war and political conflict areas—challenges and chances at the University of Sulaimani Iraqi-Kurdistan.

C. Ghaderi (✉)
Protestant University of Applied Sciences, Bochum, Germany
E-Mail: ghaderi@evh-bochum.de

1 Introduction

The reason for writing about children born of war after wartime rapes (WTR) in this paper are the Yazidi women who fell victims to ISIS crimes and gave birth to children as a result of sexualized violence in war. The existence of these children has raised human rights and ethical-normative questions. What are the points of orientation for society and law? Are they essential, according to origin and paternal line, or should they focus on a perspective of human rights and children's rights?

This article aims at exploring and conceptualizing the reality of wartime rape. What do we know from scientific research about the consequences and processes relevant for individuals and societies? And what may we learn from this for Iraq, Kurdistan and in particular for the Yazidi women, children and community?

For this purpose, I reviewed existing scientific literature, conducted interviews with experts and carried out field observations. From the results of the literature reviews and the qualitative interviews approach, psychological and psychosocial lines of consideration and, where necessary, political requirements should be derived. The survey of the situational needs and problems of the mothers and their children may demonstrate which possible interventions for post-conflict scenarios are or may be helpful.

This article aims to describe psychosocial outcomes for sexual violence survivors in order to inform future interventions. Therefore, it is divided into the following topics: 1) The prevalence, epidemiology and definitions concerning WTR, 2) explanatory approaches for WTR from a gender-sensitive perspective, 3) analyses of the multiple consequences (effects on mothers and children), transgenerational effects, transmission and the continuity of violence, and finally 4) conclusions for psychosocial interventions.

2 Wartime Rape: Prevalence, Statistics, Definitions

Prevalence. Mass rape and sexual violence continue as part of the broader strategy of conflict and war and have always been documented for wars (Njoroge 2016), including Cambodia, Liberia, Bosnia, Sierra Leone, Rwanda, Democratic Republic of Congo, Somalia, Uganda, Central African Republic, Colombia, Guinea, Iraq, Myanmar, Nigeria, South Sudan and Sudan. According to reports from the World Bank, 500,000 women were systematically raped during the 1994 genocide in Rwanda (Pankhurst 2015). In Europe, too, the issue of sexual violence in war has been prevalent. In Germany, the invasion of the Red Army at the end of the Second World War caused an estimated 1.9 million rapes. A European Community fact-finding team estimated that more than 20,000 Muslim women were raped during the war in Bosnia. During the current conflict in Iraq and Kurdistan, Yazidi girls and women are suffering. They survived the genocide and were freed from ISIS, but 13.5% of the Yazidi women became pregnant (Kizilhan 2019), with an estimated 200 children and their mothers affected.

Epidemiology. It is almost impossible to determine the precise numbers. Official statistics comprise only the tip of the iceberg of gender-based violence. According to a 2013 global study published in the American Journal of Epidemiology, only 7% of survivors of gender-based violence formally reported the violence to police, medical, or social services (Palermo et al. 2014, p. 602).

With regard to wartime rape, the estimated number of unreported cases is likely to be even higher, and the number of children is based on estimates as well. Even if persons concerned want to report, this often fails because of a lack of institutions and the structures of registration. Furthermore, rape is treated as a taboo in many contexts. In addition to tabooing and registration, questions of visibility play a role, depending on culture and war context. Is visibility given, for example of the child's biological origin as in the case of the children of GIs in Vietnam via the shape of their eyes, or of the Afro-Americans after the Second World War in Germany via their skin color? Is visibility given in the cultural context, because an unmarried woman gives birth to an illegitimate child? And is visibility given from a legal point of view because the child receives a birth certificate and is either provided with an origin, nationality and rights, or classified as being stateless and without rights?

Definition. The expression 'children born of war' is a very general term. It comprises different categories used inconsistently in scientific literature. Mochmann and Lee (2010; Mochmann 2017) distinguish four categories:

- children of foreign/enemy soldiers and local women
- children of soldiers from occupation forces and local women
- children of child soldiers
- children of UN peace-keeping forces

These categories are not absolute: As the relationship between soldiers and the civilian population in conflict and post-conflict scenarios does not follow clear or consistent patterns, a precise categorization is not always possible, and there is a grey area between so-called love relationships and relationships of dependence (Glaesmer et al. 2012). These ties may range from love relationships via friendly business arrangements, prostitution or forced prostitution, to the (systematic) violent abuse of the female population. Such different circumstances not only influence the relationship between parents, but also between mothers and their children.

In the following paragraphs I concentrate on the first category, the so-called children born of wartime rape. WTR is considered to be 'conflict-related sexual violence' (CRSV) which also includes other forms such as 'sexual slavery, forced prostitution, forced pregnancy, forced abortion, enforced sterilization, forced marriage and any other form of sexual violence of comparable gravity perpetrated against women, men, girls or boys' (UN Report 2019, p.3).

Characteristics of conflict-related sexual violence are: The perpetrators are often affiliated with a state or non-state armed group or a terrorist network. The victims are often actual or perceived members of a persecuted political, ethnic, or religious minority. And there is a climate of impunity (ibid.). Conflict-related sexual violence is now widely recognized as a war crime that is preventable and punishable. After mass rapes in Rwanda and in Bosnia and Herzegovina during the 1990s WTR has been codified as a method of warfare. According to the UN Security Council Resolution 1820 (June 2008), 'rape and other forms of sexual violence can constitute a war crime, a crime against humanity, or a constitutive act with respect to genocide' (p. 3).

3 Explanations for Wartime Rape and Sexual Violence

Even though sexualized violence against women is regularly documented in wartimes, self-explanatory theses that this violence is part of the nature of human beings or, more specifically, of men cannot be supported with scientific evidence, according to the motto 'It is wartime and therefore men will behave in this way because of men's bestial nature' (Pankhurst 2015, p. 160). Not all people rape in times of peace or war. Not all women are affected by rape. Men are also raped by other men, and in some instances even women orchestrate cases of sexualized violence against men or other women in war.

Scientific analyses demonstrate that these acts of violence can only be explained multidimensionally through individual, collective, psychological, sociological and political factors. Furthermore, these acts of violence do not always follow the same pattern, gender hierarchies and relations vary significantly across societies, and the particular pattern of rape as a practice varies across settings (Wood 2018; Pankhurst 2015, Isikozlu and Millard 2010) and is contextually and individually different. But beyond all differentiation it is certain that rape is a gendered phenomenon that cannot be analyzed without considering issues around gender. In war and crisis areas, women often become a tactical war target due to socio-cultural norms, and especially in ethno-national conflicts where the displacement or extermination of another ethnic group are central.

Gender-sensitive analyses have shown that women are symbolically construed as 'border keepers' of a nation, ethnic group or collective body. According to Mae (2010, p.727), women 'represent collective unity and identity, but also their 'honor', thus subjecting them to strict moral and cultural codes and constructing them as 'symbolic border guards', symbolic border guards of national, ethnic and cultural difference.'[1] Consequently, an attack on the women of an ethnic group constitutes the symbolic attack on the whole collective body and thus can be used as a psychological instrument of war. The position or construction of the woman as representative of a collective body is decisive, because she occupies the role of the bearer of culture and is thus associated in a symbolic way with the values of this collective body. For the reconstruction of the gendered dynamics of armed conflicts and political violence, and for viewing genocide through gendered lenses, different explanations for sexual violence in war are discussed (Apelt 2019; Pankhurst 2015; Hague 1997):

- Socio-cultural norms: patriarchal and religious values
- Rape as a weapon of war: demoralization of the 'enemy' and rape as a reward
- Masculinity as a root cause: body politics through hetero-national masculinity, militarization and territorialization of women's bodies
- Nexus between sexual violence, trafficking and terrorism

Socio-cultural norms: patriarchal and religious values
Some authors (e.g. Krenn 2003; Schick 2012; Apelt 2019) contend that socio-cultural norms defining gender roles facilitate war rape, especially patriarchal and religious values. They argue that this is true above all in patriarchal societies where masculinity is equated with dominance, power and control. Clear hierarchies are said to exist in these societies; women are subordinated and often regarded as objects whose bodies need to be protected against 'invasion'. Female bodies are the bearers of the future of the generations—in them rests not only the 'honor' of men, but also the 'honor' of a nation and culture. In many societies, it is women who are regarded as the link holding families and societies together and thus serve as a repository of social and cultural cohesion. In these societies, war rape is especially effective,

---

[1] Translation by the author.

because it destroys families, communities and, in a more general sense, cultural cohesion.

Rape as a Weapon of War: Demoralization of the 'Enemy' and Rape as a Reward

Wars are fought not only with guns, shells, tanks and drones: the female body is a battlefield as well. This intimate method of warfare harms mentally and physically. It is not uncommon that it leads to a slow death, if one considers that 'in recent wars the presence of HIV/AIDS increases the likelihood that women die as a result' (Pankhurst 2015, p. 163). Pankhurst explains the theory of rape as a weapon of war as follows:

> 'Militarised cultures and military and political leaders encourage, orchestrate and even command such acts in order to achieve two broad political outcomes. First is that of undermining the morale of the enemy communities, particular the male fighters who find themselves unable to protect their women. This is the 'rape as a weapon of war' thesis which can be found in commentaries and analyses of wars in all parts of the world and throughout history. Second is the boosting of the morale of combatants who are also said to regard rape as a reward, and also tend to bond more closely as fighters, when such violent acts against women have a collective element.' (ibid., p. 160).

In other words: rape and mass rape as a weapon in war may be part of a military or a political strategy in advance or retreat. It is classified as a persuasive military strategy for the troops to feel 'good'. Seifert (2003, p. 237) describes war rape as part of the 'Rules of War'. Her conclusion relies on several instances in history where the reward for battlefield victory was often the rape and looting of enemy women and territory.

Types of Masculinity as a Main Cause

Several authors employ terms of 'masculinity' to explain the patterns of male behavior. They argue 'that at times of socio-political tension prior to conflict, as well as during conflict itself, some types of masculinity come to be celebrated and actively promoted to a greater degree than others' (Pankhurst 2015, p. 165). In some conflict situations, the more violent aspects of masculinity are played out in all aspects of men´s lives to an extreme degree, in what Hague calls a 'hetero-national masculinity' (Hague 1997, p. 55). The dimension of masculinity in relation to national and male identities is important (ibid.) for imagined orders of nation, stability and security. Such hetero-national male identities are enforced and legitimized by means of the rape of women, their victimization and the territorialization of their bodies as war fields.

Some scholars frame gender-related oppression in other terms, for example by drawing on intersectional approaches (Crenshaw 1991), and show how gender norms and relations—what counts as appropriate masculinity and femininity—depend not just on gender roles but on other hierarchies such as race, ethnicity and class. Furthermore, there is also criticism of the justifications for gender oppression with the concept of the patriarchal gendered hierarchy. This is monocausal, ahistorical and leads to a homogenizing construction of masculinity and femininity (Patil 2013, p. 847). Gendered hierarchy is more complex. According to Wood (2018, p. 12), in 'some societies, sexual violence against those lower in the hierarchy is understood as feminizing', and in addition to that, 'The dominant -'hegemonic'- masculinity, though an ideal for many, may be realized by only a few members of society and may be contested by 'protest masculinities" (ibid.).

Nexus Between Sexual Violence, Trafficking and Terrorism
According to a 2019 UN report, a strong nexus between sexualized violence, trafficking and terrorism has developed more recently. In the process, radicalization and violent extremism have contributed to the anchoring of discriminating gender norms. Sexual assault serves strategic goals of terrorism, including the displacement of population groups, the procurement of information through interrogations, the promotion of an extremist ideology and the destabilization of social structures by means of terrorizing women and girls. Sexual assault has also been a recurring characteristic in the recruitment by groups of terrorists possibly promising young men marriage and sex slaves as forms of male rule and status. Sexual violence plays an important role in the political economy of terrorism, as physical and online slave markets as well as trafficking enable terrorist groups to earn revenue from the continuous kidnapping of women and girls (UN Report, p.6).

4 Analysis of the Multiple Consequences

Sexualized violence in war has diverse short-term and long-term, individual and social consequences for the survivors. Even though violence often occurs as mass violence, the individual experiences and ways of coping, which are different for mothers and children, should be taken into consideration.

The extent and concrete impacts are different according to their context. In the particular context of Germany after the Second World War, for example, these mothers were socially ostracized and lived in economically difficult conditions. They were single mothers or were faced with the problem to bring up a child not descending from a marriage. They did not have an opportunity for determination of paternity and maintenance claims under German law in order to get support. The living conditions of the mothers and children were characterized by social and economic deprivation, stigmatization, discrimination and exclusion (Kaiser 2015,2018).

4.1 Consequences for Women; Mothers as Victims of CRSV/WTR

There are multiple, complex and long-lasting impacts for the lives of victims, their families and their communities. Common consequences for the affected women can be summarized as follows:

- Stigma and discrimination are a common experience for survivors of WTR.
- There is the risk of unwanted pregnancy and sexually transmitted infections (including HIV/AIDS).
- CRSV/WTR happens in an acute or chronic conflict or post-conflict situation with an increased risk of other forms of traumatic events.
- Anxiety, depression and PTSD are common outcomes, and there is a high risk of developing mental disorders, especially traumatization.

It is important to know that traumatizing events can vary considerably. In the specialist literature, trauma types are classified in terms of the frequency of their occurrence (quantity), their causation, and the degree of concern (quality). Thus, short-lasting, singular accidental events such as an attack or accident are referred to as 'Accidental Mono Traumatization' or rather Type I. On the other hand, long-lasting, repeated acts of violence such as 'accumulated experiences' (Khan, 1963, p. 290) in child abuse or 'sequential' experiences, for example of war (Keilson, 1979/2005, p. 915), are subsumed under polytraumatizations or otherwise known as Type II. The implications for the latter are more diffuse, serious and complex, especially as they are intentionally inflicted on other people as so-called man-made disasters such as wartime rapes. Trauma disorders are most severely associated with man-made disaster and the degree of frequency of traumatic experiences, i.e. cumulative and sequential trauma.

4.2 Psychosocial Consequences of Children Born of Wartime Rape

Children who are born out of wartime rape are constituting a vulnerable group. This group is often denoted within the community as 'bad blood' of political, ethnical and religious enemies. These children are already stigmatized at birth and suffer their whole lives from these discriminatory consequences. Quite often, they are the chief aim for the recruitment through armed groups and terrorist organizations. Besides stigmatization and social exclusion, they are facing substantial administrative challenges regarding the registration of their birth, their legal names or their rights of citizenship.

These children are particularly at risk, because they become the symbol of the trauma of the nation as a whole and consequently, society often neglects their needs. Due to their fathers' status as the 'enemy' (Glaesmer et al. 2012, p. 321) or the 'other', children born of war are often raised in hostile environments, where they are stigmatized and discriminated against. The United Nations has recognized children born of wartime rape as particularly vulnerable to human rights abuses and developmental difficulties, because of their biological origins (UN Report 2019, p. 5).

In research and therapeutic practice, the focus has tended to be on the women, or rather the mothers, and not on the affected children. Not much attention has been given to the fact that in many societies, affiliation is defined by the fathers (family, clan, nation). Without this affiliation through a father, the children are not legitimate and therefore vulnerable, with the result that they are excluded.

Furthermore, the children are often confronted with difficult parent–child-relationships, discrimination, stigmatization and problems of identity (Glaesmer et al. 2012; Kaiser et al. 2018). In their appraisal of the psycho-social consequences for wartime children, Glaesmer et al. (2012) underline three central aspects as considerable, which they conceptualize in a model based on their survey in Germany: Identity-confusion, stigmatization and discrimination, and aversive childhood memories.

a) **Identity (-confusion):** children born of wartime rape live with a lot of open questions about identity, which mainly result from the unclear identity of their fathers. Children who grow up without their fathers experience their fatherlessness differently from children who lost their fathers during war. Sometimes they have neither memories, nor names, nor narratives of their fathers: theirs is an absolute fatherlessness: Not knowing their fathers, and knowing nothing about them, has been described by the children as the feeling that an important fragment is missing within their identity (Glaesmer et al. 2012, p. 324).

A lot of children born of wartime rape received the information about the identity of their father from their mothers later during their childhood or when they were adults. Traumatic are case histories in which children were informed about their origin by accident or through other persons. Some mothers take the secret to their graves. In post-conflict-situations many mothers withhold information about their children's fathers to protect the children, because they know that their children constitute an ideal target for racial, moral and ideological prejudices (ibid., p. 325).

b) **Stigmatization/discrimination:** For these children, open or hidden discrimination was a formative experience, as they carried a double destiny as an 'illegitimate' child and 'children of the enemy'. In Germany, 'Russian-kid' and 'Russian-brat' (Stelzl-Marx 2009, p. 352) were conventional swearwords until the 1960s. In Kurdistan they are called 'zol', which suggests that the mother had sexual intercourse with a man who was not her lawful husband. The children are also called 'mndali Na-shar-i' (منداڵی ناشەرعی), so-called illegitimate children.

c) **Aversive childhood memories:** Often, affected children live in difficult developmental conditions, for example when they grow up with their mothers among relatives. They might experience anything from emotional and physical neglect to abuse. Such violence is an expression of their mothers' ambivalence towards their children, who serve as a reminder of their rape trauma. In addition, mothers were also overwhelmed by their living conditions. A considerable number of children grew up in protectory or were given up for adoption. Other studies which also attend to the consequences for these children confirm this analysis. Van Ee and Kleber (2013), for example, identify key risk factors for children born of rape, such as strained parent–child relationships, discrimination, stigmatization, and identity issues. They argue that such children should be acknowledged as secondary rape victims and supported accordingly to minimize mental health risks. Growing up with a traumatized mother who has experienced war, death, and destruction has shown to interfere with the child's own ability to parent in the future, parental child interaction, and the psychological development of the child. Identity formation is a central stage of development during adolescence, and van Ee and Kleber's results reveal that being a young person born of rape brings with it considerable challenges. How do children born of rape handle their complex experience and react to the knowledge about their biological origin? Maybe unsurprisingly, the children feel their 'otherness' and react. Some adults who grew up in this situation stated in interviews that they had the feeling that there was something wrong with them. The situation is difficult for the children, because it is ambivalent: on the one hand, they want to have a positive relationship with their fathers, but on the other hand their father was a perpetrator who harmed their mothers. How do they find a balance between hatred and love?

Finding out about their history brings new identities for these children, which removes the previous uncertainty and at the same time renders new challenges (Hogwood 2017): once adolescents learn of their true origins, they report that what they had previously understood to be true was replaced by a different understanding, and that they constructed a new identity. In a study from Bosnia and Herzegovina (Erjavec and Volcic 2010) 19 girls born of war rape were interviewed and invited to explore how they construct their identities. The results identified key themes including experiencing a continued sense of hostility and stigma and feeling as if they belong to the 'other'. As a result, three metaphorical descriptions of their identity emerged, which were used to articulate their painful experiences:

1. Metaphor: Shooting Target

This word is taken from the semantic field of war. The interviewed girls denoted themselves as a target for repeated attacks. It shows the aggressiveness of others and the helplessness of the persons affected. It also expresses the experience of abuse and social exclusionary experiences.

2. Metaphor: Cancer

This is a biological and disease-associated term. It was not obvious to the children that they were conceived through rape, but the term points to an internalization of this knowledge of their origin and describes it as a hidden disease. In the war of Bosnia, mass rapes were part of the strategy of ethnical purge. The biological terms involve impurity and disease, because the children concerned contain within themselves 'Serbian blood'.

3. Metaphor: Warrior

Some children understand themselves as fighters for the 'good'. They use war-related terms but see themselves as active agents with a positive connotation. They see the genome inside themselves as a bridge leading away from the traumatization. This processing arises from different constructions of identity in a conceptual context of war rape.

Interesting in this context is that, 25 years after the war in Bosnia, the children of war have organized themselves and now have a public voice. The network of victims, 'Forgotten Children of War', was founded in 2016 so that those affected can help each other—just like the 'Children of the Occupation' in Germany do.

The long-term consequences for the identity of children of rape inside the ISIS war have not been evaluated so far, rather the short-term consequences are known. With regard to the recent example of Yazidi in Iraq, the following can be said: Children born during the ISIS war in Iraq and their mothers are confronted with numerous stigmata in the attempt to reintegrate into society. Some Yazidi families allow the women to return, but not their children. The spiritual leader of the Yazidi, Baba Sheikh, declared in an interview for Voice of America: 'The victims are our daughters and sisters, but it is unacceptable in our religion to allow the birth of children if both parents are no Yazidi' (Hussein 2016). As a rule, mothers live with their children in refugee camps or with members of the extended family. Because of the stigmatization, these mothers often do not reveal even to their families that the children are the product of rape. Instead, the mothers frequently tell their families that the children were born within legitimate marriages between parents who meanwhile died.

Children who were born in ISIS captivity have no civil identity documentation. They do not have access to valid birth registration and identity documentation, rendering it difficult if not impossible for them to prove their nationality and citizenship—which puts them at an increased risk of statelessness and leaves them unable to access healthcare, housing, education, and other basic services. Unregistered children are moreover exposed to a higher risk of exploitation, capture, detention and slave trade. Children who do not possess a birth certificate will also find it challenging to register marriages, deaths and births afterwards. This is a serious problem given that the rights to nationality and birth registration are fundamental rights enshrined in human rights law (Mahmood 2017).

In addition, the Iraqi law commands that the religion of the child will be determined by the religion of its father. This means that the condemnation of the children who are born out of ISIS-rapes, is maintained both by religious authority within the Yezidis society, and by Iraqi law. Furthermore, Iraqi law allows only the registration of a child´s name with the father's name. For this reason, since 2018, there has been a campaign called 'My name is my mother's name' organized by the People Development Organization (PDO) in partnership with other organizations. The aim of this campaign is to try to adjust this rule for resolving this problem. The law department at the University of Sulaimani supported the campaign with their expertise and research to receive suggestions for the Iraqi parliament (Anual Report, PDO 2018).

4.3 Transgenerational Transmission and Continuity of Violence

In trauma and attachment research (Kaiser et al. 2018), there is a broad research base comprising transgenerational effects and transmission. There is a critical discussion of the term 'transmission' which includes aspects such as the relationship between biographical and neurobiological research, or between intergenerational aspects and multigenerational aspects. These processes of trauma transmission are certainly not one-dimensional and not supra-individual. An integrative perspective should consider that socio-cultural, familial (e.g. attachment behaviour) and biological aspects influence individual development. Not only the processes, but also the substance of transmission (Kellermann 2001, 2011) have to be differentiated in transmission on self, cognition, affectivity and interpersonal functioning.

When analyzing the effects of violence, the transgenerational effects that affect individuals and family systems, as well as social continuities of violence, must be considered. In an analysis of the Yugoslav developments since 1945, Seifert (2004, p. 35) argues that the traumatic events which occurred in the Balkans during the Second World War were 'neither individually nor politically processed.' (ibid.). She argues that this 'contributed to the eruption of violence in the 90s. The post-war collective repression led to the emergence of no common social discourse that could have contributed to an understanding shared by all groups of the experiences of war.'

This overall societal and transgenerational view also becomes clear when looking at the aspects of continuity and transmission of violence: Sexual violence and attacks on women often increase in the aftermath of war. This violence comes from 'enemy' men on retreat, or even men 'on the same side', including violence from intimate partners who have returned from a front, and even those who never left. Elina Schick (2012, p. 28) argues that the issue here is not always new violence brought about by war, but the continuity of violence, which, depending on the stage of conflict, moves from the private to the public sphere. This concerns mainly women: Violence against women in conflict and post-conflict phases increases because there is a general increase in potentially violent groups and individuals such as army, non-state groups, local warlords or international troops. In addition, in so-called ethnic conflicts, there would be non-state fighters, such as Guerrilla groups. These would constitute potential perpetrators of violence without the potential for reintegration programs because they have weapons but no perspective. As a result, an increase in sexual violence can be observed: women are seen as a symbol of the state body. With the aim of demoralizing the opponent, their bodies are injured, raped, and impregnated. Therefore, mass rape in many conflicts has become a systematic weapon of war. Once the men have returned, women, who had been mobilized during the war for the labor market, are forced back into their old roles. They therefore often become subject to reprisals in uncertain post-conflict transformation phases. Furthermore, a weak constitutional state creates a general climate of impunity. These factors lead to an increase in post-war 'private' violence towards women.

Post-war periods do not necessarily lead to more peaceful times for women. Seifert (2004, p. 28) points out that 'according to observers, as a result of the use of international civilian and military peacekeepers, the sex industry in Croatia has become the country's strongest growth industry.' Even warlords are enriching themselves in post-war economies. Not infrequently women and children are negotiated as 'war material'.

That means that in addition to the continuity of violence from one generation to the next, the continuity of violence can also be seen as a continuity from private to public space, and wartime rape can be understood to be situated on a continuum of sexual violence from peace to war.

5 Conclusion for Psychosocial Interventions: Reflection on Psychosocial and Professional Interventions

Psychosocial professional interventions in post-war and conflict areas include both psychological and psychosocial help, as well as measures to restore destroyed communities and societies. Because politically motivated collective violence in war destroys both psyches and the physical world (houses, cities, villages) of people, as well as their social world (e.g. bonds and networks), it leads to the destruction of entire life and relationship contexts. In this sense, social work in post-war and conflict areas always takes place at the interface of the individual, politics and history. There is a need for individual, collective and political treatment of the violent experiences and human consequences of wars and crises.

At the same time, interventions must be considered diversely. Evidently, the same problems demand culturally different answers and psychosocial interventions. An example: The silence of the Kosovo Albanian women about rape in the war led to rash interpretations of the helpers. Local psychosocial organizations were quick to realize that Kosovar Albanian women 'did not talk' and were often quick to explain that the silence of women was due to patriarchal oppression. This unilaterally interprets women's behavior rather than capturing women's 'silence' as a strategy of trying to save the cohesion of families and communities that broke down by exposing the rape. Ignoring war-related sexual assault was a cultural coping mechanism that could also serve individual coping strategies. If helpers insisted that those affected should verbalize their experiences of violence, this could be a counterproductive way of imposing western ideas of individual psychology and problem solving.

When it comes to dealing with political traumatization processes, researchers and practitioners point out premature pathogenesis of PTSD, and rather discuss approaches to 'collective healing' than serve to secure life and community building and social work upgrading community-based approaches (see also Mlodoch 2017). These aspects are of topical importance in the analysis of the situation in Kurdistan and the Yazidi mothers and children of the war. The Yazidic women and children have received much media attention, have generated intense feelings among us all, from compassion for the women and their families, to fear of the perpetrators. As inconceivably 'bestial' as the phenomenon is, it is to be expected in specific temporal contexts when we analyze the causes from a transnational, gender-sensitive and process-oriented perspective, consider the multiple consequences for mothers and children, and reflect psychosocial interventions from a transgenerational perspective.

The evaluations of my own qualitative interviews and field observations have revealed that there is a clear ambivalence between women and the community regarding the demand for 'opening': A community that has genocidal experiences and was traditionally 'closed' faces the challenge and the expectation of opening up to the wounded women and their children whose fathers are the 'enemy'.

What do we deduce from these findings? The following perspectives are necessary for the analysis:

a) A transnational and contextual perspective on WTR is helpful for describing the phenomenon and makes it easier to identify general and specific aspects.
b) A process-oriented perspective regarding children and mothers widens the view of life, development and the multiple consequences that mothers and children have to bear.
c) A process-oriented perspective, which perceives the continuity of violence in society, is a subject-oriented, empowering perspective, which hears the voice of those affected and gives space to them. It does not instrumentalize them, because those affected are defined by more than the violence that they have experienced.

References

Apelt, M. (2019). Militär und Krieg: der kämpfende Mann, die friedfertige Frau und ihre Folgen. In B. Kortendiek, B. Riegraf, & K. Sabisch (Eds.), *Handbuch Interdisziplinäre Geschlechterforschung. Geschlecht und Gesellschaft* (Vol. 65). Wiesbaden: Springer VS. https://doi.org/10.1007/978-3-658-12496-0_57.

Crenshaw, K. (1991). Mapping the margins intersectionality, identity politics, and violence against women of color. *Stanford Law Review, 43,* 1241–1299.

Erjavec, K., & Volcic, Z. (2010). Living with the sins of their fathers: An analysis of self-representation of adolescents born of war rape. *Journal of Adolescent Research, 25,* 359–386.

Glaesmer, H. (2019). Langzeitfolgen der traumatischen Erfahrungen aus dem Zweiten Weltkrieg in der deutschen älteren Bevölkerung. *Ärztliche Psychotherapie, 14,* 85–91.

Glaesmer, H., Kaiser, M., Freyberger, H. J., Brähler, E., & Kuwert, P. (2012). Die Kinder des Zweiten Weltkrieges in Deutschland—Ein Rahmenmodell für die psychosoziale Forschung. *Trauma & Gewalt, 6*(4), 318–328.

Hague, E. (1997). Rape, power and masculinity: The construction of gender and national identities in the war in Bosnia-Herzegovina. In R. Lentin (Ed.), *Gender and Catastrophe* (pp. 50–63). Gender and catastrophe, New York: Zed Books.

Hogwood, J., Mushashi, C., Jones, S., & Auerbach, C. (2017). 'I learned who i am': Young people born from genocide rape in rwanda and their experiences of disclosure. *Journal of Adolescent Research, 1,* 22.

Hussein, R. (2016). Voice of America, 20 August 2016. https://www.voanews.com/extremism-watch/pregnant-rape-victims-face-challenges-upon-returning-iraq.

Isikozlu, E., & Millard, A. (2010). Towards a typology of wartime rape (Brief series No. 43). Bonn: BICC.

Kaiser, M., Kuwert, P., Brähler, E., & Glaesmer, H. (2018). Long-term effects on adult attachment in German occupation children born after World War II in comparison with a birth-cohort-matched representative sample of the German general population. *Aging Mental Health, 22,* 197–207.

Kaiser, M., Kuwert, P., & Glaesmer, H. (2015). Aufwachsen als Besatzungskind des Zweiten Weltkrieges in Deutschland—Hintergründe und Vorgehen einer Befragung deutscher Besatzungskinder. *Zeitschrift Für Psychosomatische Medizin Und Psychotherapie, 61*(2), 191–205.

Keilson, H. (2005). Sequentielle Traumatisierung bei Kindern. Untersuchung zum Schicksal jüdischer Kriegswaisen (pp. 915–926). Gießen: Psychosozial-Verlag (First publication 1979).

Kellermann, N. P. F. (2001). Transmission of Holocaust Trauma—An Integrative View. Psychiatry: Interpersonal and Biological Processes. Vol. 64, September, pp. 256–267.

Kellermann, N. P. F. (2011). ‚Geerbtes Trauma'. Die Konzeptualisierung der transgenerationellen Weitergabe von Traumata. *Tel Aviver Jahrbuch für deutsche Geschichte 39,* 137–160.

Krenn, R. (2003). Krieg, Militär und Geschlechterverhältnis. In Frauen und Militarismus. Frauen Gesellschaft Kritik. Centaurus Verlag & Media: Herbolzheim. https://doi.org/10.1007/978-3-86226-826-9_4.

Khan, M. M. (1963). The concept of cumulative trauma. *Psychoanalytic Study of the Child, 18,* 286–306.

Kizilhan, J. (2019). Fünf Jahre nach dem Völkermord an Yeziden. Eine Bestandsaufnahme und Handlungsempfehlungen. Ed. GfbV (Gesellschaft für bedrohte Völker).

Mae, M. (2010). Nation, Kultur und Gender: Leitkategorien der Moderne in Wechselbeziehung. In R. Becker & B. Kortendiek (Eds.), *Handbuch Frauen- und Geschlechterforschung* (pp. 724–730). Wiesbaden: Springer.

Mahmood, S. (2017). Challenges of children born by ISIS rape in Iraq. https://www.cerahgeneve.ch/files/1715/0963/3793/WP49-Challenges-Children-Born-by-ISIS-Rape-Iraq.pdf.

Mlodoch, K. (2017). *Gewalt, Flucht—Trauma?—Grundlagen und Kontroversen der psychologischen Traumaforschung.* Göttingen: Reihe FluchtAspekte.

Mochmann, I. C. (2017). Children born of war—A decade of international and interdisciplinary research. *Historical Social Research, 42*(1), 320–346. https://doi.org/https://doi.org/10.12759/hsr.42.2017.1.320-346.

Mochmann, I. C., & Lee, S. (2010). The Human Rights of Children Born of War: Case Analyses of Past and Present Conflicts. *Historical Social Research, 35*(3), 268–298.

Njoroge, F. (2016). Evolution of rape as a war crime and a crime against humanity. SSRN: https://ssrn.com/abstract=2813970.

Palermo, T., Bleck, J., Peterman, A. (2014). Tip of the iceberg: Reporting and gender-based violence in developing countries. *American Journal of Epidemiology, 179*(5), 1 March 2014, 602–612.

Patil, V. (2013). From patriarchy to intersectionality: A transnational feminist assessment of how far we've really come. *Signs, 38*(4), 847–867.

Pankhurst, D. (2015). Sexual violence in war. In Shepherd, Laura J. Gender Matters in Global Politics. A feminist introduction to international relations. 2. Edition, published by Routledge, pp. 159–171.

Schick, E. (2012). NGOs in Krisengebieten. Herausforderungen frauenpolitischer NGOs in Post-Conflikt-Situationen. Bonner Studien zum globalen Wandel. Band 17.

Seifert, R. (2004). Soziale Arbeit und kriegerische Konflikte. Band 12. Lit-Verlag.

Seifert, R. (2003). Im Tod und im Schmerz sind nicht alle gleich: Männliche und weibliche Körper in der kulturellen Anordnung von Krieg und Nation. In S. Martus, M. Münkler, & W. Röcke (Eds.), *Schlachtfelder* (pp. 235–247). Codierung von Gewalt im medialen Wandel: Akademie Verlag.

Security Council Resolution. 1820, U.N. Doc. S/RES/1820 (June 19, 2008), https://undocs.org/en/S/1820(2008).

Stelzl-Marx, B. (2009). Die unsichtbare Generation: Kinder sowjetischer Besatzungssoldaten in Österreich und Deutschland. *Historical Social Research, 34*(3), pp. 352–372. https://doi.org/https://doi.org/10.12759/hsr.34.2009.3.352-372.

UN Report Conflict Related Sexual Violence. (2019). https://www.un.org/sexualviolenceinconflict/wp-content/uploads/2019/04/report/s-2019-280/Annual-report-2018.pdf.

Van Ee, E., & Kleber, R. J. (2013). Growing up under a shadow: Key issues in research on and treatment of children born of rape. *Child Abuse Review, 22*(3), 386–397.

Wood, E. J. (2018). Rape as a practice of war: Toward a typology of political violence, Politics & Society. pp. 1–25.

The Refugee as a Stigmatized Individual – Spoiled Identities, Possible Causes and Courses of Action for Social Work

Lisa-Marie Dünnebacke and Kristin Goetze

Abstract

Due to their special residence status, refugees are partially or completely excluded from many areas of social life. This article examines the social exclusion of refugees by referring to Goffman's stigma theory and the question if flight can be understood as a stigma and, if so, what its specific characteristics are. According to the authors, the special value of stigma theory lies in the fact that it allows for an investigation into the consequences of exclusion for the self-image of refugees and their everyday survival strategies without falling into individualizing interpretations of a socially induced crisis. For social work that might take place in post-war and political conflict areas, an analysis of causes of social exclusion is constitutive. The social justice approach will be introduced briefly as one option for this analysis to decouple monologic modes of thought and to differentiate a – so-called – transcultural competence.

Keywords

Stigma • Refugee • Spoiled identities • Social justice • Communication • Discrimination

L.-M. Dünnebacke (✉) · K. Goetze
Protestant University of Applied Sciences, Bochum, Deutschland
E-Mail: l.duennebacke@outlook.com

K. Goetze
E-Mail: KristinGoetze@gmx.de

Preface

The fact that refugees are affected by material and social exclusion is undisputed in scientific literature; as a particular *legal construct*, refugees are in many respects denied exercising their rights – with harsh consequences for their lives.[1] Given the seemingly obvious nature of this problem, the question might arise whether it is worth dealing with the stigmatization of refugees at all – would it not be more important to talk about the causes of flight and the political strategies of refugee policy?

Analysing and discussing this question is indeed necessary. However, the social exclusion and stigmatization of refugees continue to exist, so that especially social work – as a profession that has to deal with social exclusion of refugees on a daily basis – is confronted with the challenge of developing an attitude towards this issue. This article takes the perspective of Goffman's stigma theory as a basis and develops some thoughts on its reception regarding the research of flight. In addition, the article attempts to build on Goffman´s stigma theory by drawing on the so-called Social Justice and Diversity concept (Czollek et al. 2019) in order to trace the development of analyses over time, and the different approaches to dealing with stigmatization. The relevance of context and time will become apparent from those approaches.

1 Stigma – a Social Relationship

In the original literal sense, a stigma denotes a burn or wound mark; the term has, however, been used for a long time in religious contexts, or as a description of physical characteristics such as disease-related deformities. In his 1963 article *Stigma. Notes on the Management of Spoiled Identities*, Erving Goffman developed a different understanding of the term, which is based on a moral interpretation. According to this, a stigma is an attribute of a person that has a negative connotation and marginalizes the subject (cf. Olk 2017, p. 930).

The processes of stigmatization arise from the fact that society categorizes people on the basis of socially coded values and norms, and ascribes certain characteristics to these categories. This is a process of social interaction, which

---

[1] The status of a refugee and its consequences are highly dependent on the specific situation in the country he/she lives in; this article is based on the situation in Germany.

requires orientation points through actions and a shared communication system based on similar subcultural affiliations.[2] In social interaction, a person has categories assigned to them, including the associated attributes (virtual social identity). These attributions and expectations may well differ from what the person actually *is*, their nature and character (their actual self-constructed identity). In this context, a stigma is a characteristic that degrades the person. Virtual and actual social identity become separated, and the person is labeled (cf. Goffman 1963, pp. 10). Codes, which build upon this characteristic and – after reproducing this stigma, lead to a stereotype – differentiate between the *'normals'*[3] (the so-called *us*) and the *'others'*; this process is called *othering* and produces feelings of security through a subliminal hierarchy process, which can establish itself as a norm and consolidate, depending on the context, into structural discrimination (cf. Czollek et al. 2019, pp. 26).

Therefore, the degrading and exclusionary character of a stigma must be noted: an individual who could be accepted by the social community is excluded because of a striking characteristic. It is important to emphasize that this does not happen because of the characteristics themselves. In a different context and social circle, the same characteristic can be experienced as a normal quality and not lead to exclusion (cf. Goffman 1963, pp. 4). The characteristic *mobility*, for example, is connoted positively in contexts of professional opportunities, but then turns into a stigma – a negative characteristic – in the context of Romani culture, because it deviates from the *normal* way of privileged living. A stereotype – once formed – provides fertile ground for an othering process.

A stigma has a variety of manifestations. It can refer to a physical characteristic in the form of physical abnormalities, such as amputations or malformities of the body. Another type is a stigma which associates individual character traits with negative connotations. Thus, a lack of willpower or dishonesty, which are characteristics associated with certain social positions, such as that of the early school leaver or a prostitute, can act as a stigma. Here, it becomes particularly clear that the stigma itself can initiate a downward dynamic: Because a person has a characteristic that is negatively connoted, he or she is also assigned further negative attributes that are attached to this stigma. In Germany, a highly

---

[2] The idea of a pre-judgement also has a positive function in social interaction in a society; it stabilizes and structures the communication between its members (cf. Olk 2017, 930 ff.).

[3] When we use the word 'normal', it is not including judgements or labeling; we refer to Goffman's terminology (1963); first mentioned on p. 5.

performance-oriented society, an example could be unemployment: The unemployed are often stigmatized as uneducated, lazy or socially neglected (cf. Krug et al. 2019).

A third category that is particularly relevant for this article is that of so-called *phylogenetic* characteristics, amongst which Goffman counts stigmatization processes based on gender, ethnicity, religion or social class.

Even if there are various types of stigma and concepts, or maybe terms for this process, they all show the same sociological feature: They turn the person who possesses the stigma into a discredited person, and all their other characteristics become irrelevant. By stigmatizing someone, 'we exercise varieties of discrimination, through which we effectively, if often unthinkingly, reduce his life chances' (cf. Goffman 1963, p. 5).

The most comprehensive analysis of discrimination structures is based on the Social Justice and Diversity concept (cf. Czollek et al. 2019). Within this framework, the authors Czollek, Perko and Weinbach differentiate between three levels of structural discrimination – the individual, the cultural and the institutionalized level, which is, however, still in process and based on the institutional level. Most cases can be located on each of these levels at the same time, although this depends on the time and context. None of the levels is worse than any of the others– there is no hierarchy intended.

The individual level is based on personal standing, actions, activities and speech acts, which make behaviours identified as stereotypical obvious and give a space to strengthening and reproducing them. The cultural level frames social roles, music, art, literature, rituals and languages, and leads to the same process as mentioned above. On the institutional level, politics, law and organizational structures give rise to stereotypes and disadvantage people. The institutionalized level is the most unpredictable and least changeable of these, because the stereotypes produced here have a normative character as they are already enshrined within the laws, which produces a feeling of certainty. Since those are written down, it is even harder to change them and interrupt the reproducing process.

The expectations mentioned above occur through communicative processes, which contribute to achieving the most 'effective' norm that guarantees the continuity of society. Moreover, this norm minimizes the complexity of the new and unknown – the 'other' – to structure society according to a normative schema. Within this schema, it is clear who the 'privileged' ones are and who the 'others' are. Everything new or other heightens the sense of uncertainty, and represents the possibility in this society to shift towards an unprivileged position.

These communication processes – fully formed by language and interaction – are building on the intertwined actions of different communication systems, which are relevant for the framing system – like politics, law or family. These very systems are functional, contribute to the continuity of current society and benefit it (cf. Habermas and Luhmann 1971, p. 24). So how can something be changed that is formed by a functional system – like politics?

As mentioned at the beginning, the thesis of this article is that the status of a 'refugee' is in itself a stigma. It is therefore necessary to analyse how this status develops, manifests itself and is used in language. For – as the preceding assertion states – the status of a refugee is neither natural nor objective, but rather legally and politically constructed – with existential consequences for the lives of those affected.

2   The Stigma of Being a Refugee

When exploring processes of exclusion and stigmatization of refugees, one is inevitably confronted with the question of how a definition of this group can be achieved at all. This is a challenge, because the issue is legally complex and socially controversial. The 1951 Geneva Refugee Convention and the corresponding article of the German Basic Law define a refugee as a person seeking protection from political persecution.[4] The first legal label for refugees therefore relates to their reasons for flight. It means that people who leave their country due to material need and poverty, or lack of health care, *cannot be* refugees. Consequently, at least in the German media debate, a fundamental distinction is made between 'accepted' refugees and so-called 'poverty-migrants', who are 'only' in the country to find work and to live more comfortably. The allocation to a certain category is decisive for the social integration opportunities of refugees and the extent to which they are socially accepted.

The distinction between 'good' and 'bad' refugees is reflected, for example, in the political construction of the 'Bleibeperspektive' ('prospect of remaining'), which describes how likely a refugee is to remain in Germany. In German asylum policy, refugees are given the opportunity to obtain a positive decision regarding their application for asylum and a legal residence permit. This currently means

---

[4] According to the Geneva Convention on Refugees, a person can be considered a refugee, if he or she „*owing to well-founded fear of being persecuted for reasons of race, religion, nationality, membership of a particular social group or political opinion, is outside the country of his nationality [...]"* (cf. Art.1 of Convention and protocol Text of the 1951 Convention Relating to the Status of Refugees).

According to Art. 16a (1) Grundgesetzes „*Politically persecuted persons enjoy right of asylum*".

that only refugees with 'good' prospects of staying in Germany have access to an integration course during the application process. The accommodation during the asylum procedure is significantly worse if a refugee has 'poor' prospects of staying.[5] According to the definition of the Federal Office for Migration and Refugees (BAMF), whether a refugee has good or bad prospects of staying is determined according to whether they come from a country of origin where the overall protection rate exceeds 50%. The political desire to exclude refugees from opportunities for social integration is revealed clearly: When assessing the integration 'capacity' of refugees, the BAMF refers to a construct (the 'Bleibeperspektive'), the basis of which – the overall protection rate – was created by the BAMF itself. This is because the BAMF examines and decides on asylum applications and the achievement of an overall protection quota (cf. BAMF 2019a; BAMF 2019b). The stigma of the refugee status and its exclusionary character is therefore first established by law, which is another functional system. In this case – because of its written character – the institutionalized level of structural discrimination might take effect and consolidate this stigmatized norm of status, which is an ascribed attribute. A refugee with this status therefore falls outside of the settled normative schema and becomes *the other*.

3 Initial Conclusions

The previous remarks have, at least rudimentarily, addressed the social framing of the stigmatization of refugees. This seems indispensable, since the effect of a stigma and the confrontation with the affected group cannot be considered without recognizing the origin of the stigma itself. And even if the debate about refugee status has only been taken up recently, it should be clear that 'the refugee' is a *political* and *legal* construct, which exhibits a political will to exclude. This shows that in the context of politically enlightened social work, which deals with the consequences of wars and conflicts, an examination of the stigmatization of refugees that remains at the level of individual coping and processing would be

---

[5] In 2018, the government of North Rhine-Westphalia established the „Steps of asylum"-plan. Its aim: Only refugees with a good perspective for staying are allowed to move into the communities. All others need to stay in the central stations of the county – they are not allowed to work, children are not going to school, they have less access to health care and are not allowed to drive to any places they want, e.g. to visit their family (cf. Ministery for children, families, refugees and integration 2018). As we can see: The possibilities for integration and participation in German society are mainly determined by this construct.

too short-sighted. When we talk about discriminated groups such as refugees, we need to keep in mind that.

> '[…] sociologically, the central issue concerning these groups is their place in the social structure; the contingencies these persons encounter in face-to-face interaction is only one part of the problem, and something that cannot itself be fully understood without reference to the history, the political development, and the current policies of the group' (cf. Goffman 1963, p. 128).

4   Consequences of the Stigmatization of Refugees: Spoiled Identities

As outlined above, a stigma not only leads to material social exclusion for those affected, but also has consequences for their self-image. Often the stigmatized individual internalizes the standards and values of society – the same standards by which they fail:

> 'His deepest feelings about what he is may be his sense of being a normal person, a human being like anyone else, a person, therefore, who deserves a fair chance and a fair break. […] Yet he may perceive, usually quite correctly, that whatever others profess, they do not really accept him and are not ready to make contact with him on equal grounds. Further, the standards he has incorporated from the wider society equip him to be intimately alive to what others see as his failing, inevitably causing him, if only for moments, to agree that he does indeed fall short of what he really ought to be' (cf. Goffman 1963, p. 7).

In their dealings with institutions such as the Foreigners Authority or the Job Centre, refugees experience directly that their status is associated with devaluation. It can also be assumed that they experience exclusion in everyday social interactions, although there is limited research in this area. If individuals thus directly experience the rejection already conveyed to them through institutional guidelines, language, actions and interactions (the 'othering' process), then, according to Goffman, the result can be a split between the 'ideal' of the self and the self (cf. ibid., pp. 8). This means that individuals begin to accept the negative connotation of their own qualities as something harmful attached to them. This process of adopting the attribution of others in one's self-conception is not deterministic, but it is nevertheless unsurprising, since refugees and their consciousness are often a product of modern societies and share the standards by which they supposedly cannot prove themselves.

To exemplify this: When a child is born and the midwife – based on the child's biological characteristics, her known expectations and, in this scenario, in line with socially established heteronormativity – exclaims that 'It is a boy!' (or a girl), then this is a social construct as well. Consequently, a process is initiated, which ascribes indirectly a specific gendered identity that is accepted by the respective society. With one verbal invocation, a set of gendered expectations is imposed on the individual, and with it the person is exposed to the possibility of being socially excluded should they not fulfil these expectations later in life (cf. Plößer 2013, p. 201; Dünnebacke 2018, p. 3).

5 Dealing with Stigmatization: Obstinacy, Passing and Techniques of Information Control

The stigmatized individual must find a way to cope in a 'normal' society. According to Goffman, in the process of overcoming a stigma, there is no inconsiderable difference between a stigma that was acquired at birth and a stigma acquired later in life, as the example above also illustrates.

In the case of refugees, the latter is the case: They have usually experienced some form of recognition in their home society, unless they have fled on grounds of discrimination. But even if belonging to a minority or sexual orientation already attached a form of stigma to them before, with their arrival in Germany and the legal status assignment, they are confronted with a new or previously unknown stigma. Thus, dealing with this new stigma is an extended 'challenge'. This is called an intersectional process, which shows that social norms cannot be conceptualized without considering other ascriptions. Therefore, it is important to analyze correlations and synergies between these categories of discrimination to see the underlying structure (cf. Walgenbach 2007; 2011). This inevitably raises the question of how the subject behaves in the face of such negative attributions and the associated social exclusion, and what strategies a person develops regarding their 'stigma- management' (cf. Goffman 1963, 99).

According to Goffman, an important strategy is so-called 'passing', i.e. the concealment or disguising of information about the corresponding stigma. For a stigmatized person, learning to 'pass' is an almost inevitable part of their socialization and moral development, since the advantages of discarding the stigma and passing as 'normal' are too great. For refugees, the particular difficulty with this form of information control regarding their own identity lies in the fact that their stigma has been *institutionally* established. The asylum procedure, registration, central accommodation – all these are elements of a stigmatization process in which the power of the institution has a discrediting effect on refugees, even after they have left the foreigners authority or after they have successfully completed the asylum procedure (cf. ibid., pp. 93). Thus, the personal identity of refugees, including their stigmatization, is expressed in a kind of institutionalized symbolism, starting with the name on their identity papers. These kinds of symbolic documents, which formalise the stigma, are especially relevant in the case of refugees – their identity papers define who they are and what their opportunities in this society are; and at the same time the papers limit their self-presentation:

> 'Whether an individual's biographical life line is sustained in the minds of his intimates or in the personnel files of an organization, and whether the documentation of his personal identity is carried on his person or stored in files, he is an entity about which a record can be built up – a copybook has been made ready for him to blot' (ibid., pp. 62 .).

As a consequence, it may happen that over the course of an individual's life they become aware that this strategy of 'passing' is no longer fruitful, and the person loses the desire to conceal the stigma. Such a transformation often manifests itself in the expression of the struggle to regain dignity: The recognition as a person with – or despite – stigma is fundamentally important to the subject (cf. Brandmeier 2019; Hollstein et al. 2010).

Even if the word 'passing' may have a negative connotation and suggests the idea that the subject deliberately and consciously deceives others, Goffman's term is by no means meant to be derogatory – on the contrary: it seems inevitable for the stigmatized subject to develop such strategies in order to come to terms with a foreign attribution and the social exclusion over which the individual has no influence. The moralizing condemnation of refugees who, for example, try to conceal their origin by preferring to remain silent rather than to show a lack of linguistic ability, is above all one thing: a mechanism by which the 'normal' moralize the coping strategies of the stigmatized in order to keep them supposedly legitimized in their assigned social place (cf. Goffman 1963, pp. 87).

Another strategy to deal with the stigma is a changed, stubborn interpretation of one's own situation. Refugees turn their back on the social standards by which they fail and try to assert their own social identity against the negative attributions of others. A strategy directly opposed to this is reflected in attempts at 'correcting' oneself in order to fit in with society. A classic example of this in the field of migration and flight is an overemphasis on the will to perform. Those who make a particular effort and learn a lot can, despite their stigma of having a migration background, manage to climb the social ladder – contrary to all predictions (cf. El-Mafaalani 2012).

All in all, the stigmatized individual is confronted with the need to control what information about their stigma is going public. The strategies described above can be observed in the field of flight, even if these topics have, so far, only been marginally explored. Therefore, deception, stubbornness or self-correction should be understood as a necessity for the subjects – they all should be a criticism of society, not of the individuals who must apply these strategies.

6 Critical Self-Reflection of Professional Help

The question now arises how professional social work can deal with the knowledge of the stigmatization of refugees and their influence on identity formation. For that, it becomes apparent in the social contact with refugees that a critical self-reflection of the professionals is urgently needed, since certain ideas of what 'helps' lead to behaviour that is at the very least questionable. Professional social work (and political institutions) should not merely advise refugees – in stark contrast to their experience of being marginalized – to see themselves as valuable human beings. Exclusion is not in itself denied, but it is argued that exclusions are only *parts* of social life and that in other areas the refugee is indeed like everyone else (cf. Goffman 1963, p. 15). This kind of advice can be helpful, but one should be aware that it also includes the logic of '[…] a formula for handling normals' (ibid., p. 116). According to this 'formula' the stigmatized individual is advised to be patient and understanding when confronted with the behaviour of the normals. The refugee should understand that it is hard for the normals to get used to the other; by considering himself or herself as normal, the stigmatized individual supports the rest of society in doing the same:

> 'It is said that if he is really at ease with his differentness, this acceptance will have an immediate effect upon normals, making it easier for them to be at ease with him in social situations. In brief, the stigmatized individual is advised to accept himself as a normal person because of what others can gain in this way, and hence likely he himself, during face-to-face interaction. The line inspired by normals, then, obliges the stigmatized individual to protect normals in various ways' (ibid., p. 120).

The strategy for dealing with exclusion suggested here to refugees is therefore to adopt the norms and values that are already prevailing in the host society. Before this background the idea of what integration should be must be criticized:

> 'The nature of a good adjustment is now apparent. It requires that the stigmatized individual cheerfully and unselfconsciously accept himself as essentially the same as normals, while at the same time he voluntarily withholds himself from those situations in which normals would find it difficult to give lip service to their similar acceptance of him' (ibid., p. 122).

Refugees are requested to assimilate to a society which does not accept them and which makes them excluded persons in the first place. The stigmatized individual is invited to find a conciliatory way of dealing with the mechanisms which separate them from work, education, health and family. The irony of this position is not that the refugee patiently tries to find a way into society. Rather, the contradictoriness of most integration requirements lies in the fact that if the stigmatized individual actually wants to live and be accepted '*as it is*', so that for example their refugee status – the stigma – is to become irrelevant, then they achieve the best chances of success, by orienting themselves towards marginalizing social standards. And so it happens that the best assimilation and integration strategy for refugees is usually even more beneficial to the host society (cf. ibid., p. 152).

Therefore, we propose a critical reflection of the structures that work for the 'normals'. This means that social work expands its repertoire of actions by an important factor: In addition to relationship work and individual care (which are undoubtedly necessary), an analysis of the political structures and their influence in social interaction is necessary. One approach for this can be the social justice and diversity concept.

7 The Social Justice- and Diversity-Concept – an Opportunity to Decouple Monologic Modes of Thought

A problem with the above-mentioned strategy of social work is that, as said before, only functional systems can differentiate a norm and negotiate it. The underlying encoding must contribute to the continuity of the existing society and must bring a benefit. That is why politics, law and indeed family are the main function systems in German society (cf. Dünnebacke 2019, pp. 35). Since social work is not necessary for everybody and determined by social policy resources – and therefore restricted in its autonomy – (cf. Klassen 2004, pp. 151), it cannot be a functional system and it cannot contribute to the continuity of the existing society directly. That is why social work can only take an advisory role and operate in reactive or compensatory ways. Thus, social work just tries to balance exclusion effects instead of combating exclusion and conveying inclusion.

Considering Klassen's illustration of the reasons why social work is limited in its impact: How can social work nevertheless get into a position where it can take at least an indirect function and exert an influence on the encoding of ascribed negative characteristics?

As outlined above, such encoding processes of stigma and of norms are socially induced by expectations. So, one might argue, they are actually changeable.

Such expectations occur through communicative processes, which contribute to achieving the most 'effective' norm – the norm which guarantees the continuity of society. These communication processes are building on intertwined actions of communication bearers, who have relevant attributes for the framing system.

Crucial points are thus the communication process, and an awareness of the communicative actions undertaken within systems like politics and law, which frame and code the status of refugees. Those actions are the 'what' and the 'how' in a society, they create and support all systems and their subsystems. They are the knowledge, faith, morals, and customs, and the habits of people which are implemented in whichever way. Or, as Dünnebacke (2019) illustrates when referring to Othman (2013), they are building up the culture of each society as the entirety of a society's mental, social and creative legacy which can be compared – on a metaphorical level – with a heart as the security of all organs (cf. ibid., p. 22).

To be aware of this sum of communications between all (sub-)systems and hence of the functional ones, it is crucial for social workers to practice a conscious existence – *conscious* through theoretically acquired knowledge and *existence* through presence in practice. A foundation for this can be the so-called *Mahloquet*[6] – a dialogue, mediation and communication method linked to the social justice and diversity concept. The method reaches back to the Jewish tradition of interpreting religious texts and was modified accordingly. In addition to the analyses of discriminatory structures, it is important to go beyond the structural categorization of an individual in order to recognize those persons beyond their established diversity category. Therefore, this method – as the foundation for the position just mentioned – is a dialogic interlocutory form as well as an ethical-dialogic attitude, which enables an equal pluralism of perspectives (cf. Czollek et al. 2019, pp. 51). This is why it is also called a dialogical contention. This is

---

[6]The normative frame of references is provided through non-violence and the UN Declaration of Human Rights (cf. Czollek et al. 2019, 51).

not about synthesizing different positions, not about a consensus of perspectives and not about monologic modes of thinking and acting, but about the possibility to allow different perspectives to stand side by side, without a right or wrong – basically, everything is instead considered new or unknown. Everybody has the right to speak – or not to speak. In order to gain insights and to broaden the context, it is important to keep asking questions until the whole perspective has been understood as far as possible – this is the distinction of the new without projecting one's own experiences and without using the other person as an alter ego. This is how the systemic-intersectional perspective with its specific language and pictures can be deconstructed, in order to distinguish the similarity and intersection between characteristics, norms and therefore different forms of structural discrimination. It is thus important to be aware of the stigma, but not to talk about and focus on it. The difference between this and other empowerment areas, where only one perspective of the persons affected by a stigma is considered, lies in the focus on more than just one perspective. This opens the possibility for everybody to be heard with equal weight, so people can reflect and expand on their own presuppositions and knowledge without precluding other perspectives and norms. In this way, a conscious existence can be achieved without expanding a hierarchy.

The method is characterized by the following aspects: conversations are on-topic, there is no list of speakers, nobody is heard first due to, for example, their status, one's own self is not the focus of conversations, rather the personal conversation, emotions and thoughts of other persons should be realized, and historical and actual perceptions are included.

These aspects can be made possible by communicating the background of questions and connections, and by practicing active listening where the content is not interpreted within the framework of one's own experiences, and where questions are asked until the perspective of the other person has been completely understood. Through asking, the process is slowed down and it becomes easier to open up new perspectives (cf. ibid.).

At first it might sound easy to implement such a process of communication, but this is not how communication usually works in society. Normally, there must be a 'right' or a 'wrong', an A or a B, an induced norm to explain the individual behaviour in front of a hierarchy structure.

This strategy makes it possible to extend the knowledge of the dynamic of actions – and therefore culture – in order to deconstruct an essentialist (homogeneous/concluded) understanding and changes it into a processual and transcultural understanding. It is indeed not easy to adopt this process in order to change a functional system like politics, but it is nevertheless important to raise questions – repeatedly – about the relevance of this specific status. Social workers do not need to occupy a more senior position for this, they just need more attachment to institutions implemented as subsystems within the political system, for example. This is how social work can disrupt indirectly without losing the relationship between the individual and their professionality in work processes. Since they might raise their voices within political systems, they then also get a political voice and will acquire negotiating power. However, this requires to be present in practice, knowing about the surrounding networks and expanding one's knowledge depending on context and time. Raising questions and collaborating with other networks creates a wider scope of action. This does not mean that the status becomes irrelevant, but the options of dealing with it are becoming more varied. Often, the unkown is the reason why those bearing such a stigma are rejected and why only compensatory reactions are possible. But to work in the mode of *Mahloquet* enables people to focus on more than just the status – by using other resources –, but still to monitor and combat the exclusionary effects and therefore to convey inclusion. The relationship with the client is thus based on the idea of being allies, as a living solidarity in a position of non-positioning.

Finally, a practical example: A woman fled with her daughter from Iran to Germany, and now has a residence permit. The current social worker told her, in every meeting, that the foreigners registration office is obliged to issue her an electronic card for her residence permit – the social worker did not look properly at the context, time and current information, and projected his feelings of perplexity to the woman. The social worker certainly did not know that she had to renew her paper permit three times in a row, and fulfil different requirements, because he did not ask. The woman thought – and this was obviously a communication problem – that the electronic card would entitle her to more money for her daughter and money for setting up her flat. She expected more privileges and felt discriminated and resigned when these did not materialize. The actual problem was, as it turned out, that the previous social worker had not helped her to apply for child benefit and residential allowance. After applying for those grants, the electronic card itself and the attached status were not as important anymore. Once this has been resolved, she has the feeling of security and can focus on other important issues. This has been achieved just by looking at other intersections, being allied as a living solidarity in a position of non-positioning – which means also to reflect on one's own projection of feelings.

The example shows that it is always important to raise questions: is there any disadvantage for already privileged people, and are there any other possibilities to achieve this more privileged status – maybe by working on other intersections?

8 Consequences

Without repeating the thoughts and arguments above, the main conclusion from Goffman's theory and the concept of social justice may be this: the attribution of what is normal and what is not, the structures of discrimination and social exclusion, are factual. It seems 'natural' that a certain norm is valid, as if it were a real thing with the same substance as a person. However, it should be emphasized that these kinds of attribution processes are by no means natural or given. In fact, they are socially induced due to expectations and therefore can certainly be changed. Hence, the question is not if we can change them, but rather, how, when, and who should do it.

As a consequence, we propose a critical reflection of the structures that work for the 'normal' and privileged members of the society in which a refugee arrives. This means that social work expands its repertoire of actions by an important factor: In addition to relationship work and individual care (which is undoubtedly necessary), an analysis of the political structures and their influence in social interaction is necessary. One approach for this can be the social justice and diversity concept.

References

Aumüller, J. (2008). Kommunale Flüchtlingsintegration in Schwäbisch Hall. In J. Aumüller & C. Bretl (Eds.), *Lokale Gesellschaften und Flüchtlinge: Förderung von sozialer Integration. Die kommunale Integration von Flüchtlingen in Deutschland* (pp. 109–139). Berlin: Edition Parabolis.

Bundesamt für Migration und Flüchtlinge (BAMF). (2019a). Gesamtschutzquote: Anteil der als Flüchtling oder asylberechtigt anerkannten Asylbewerber in Deutschland von 2005 bis 2019. Statista GmbH. https://de.statista.com/statistik/daten/studie/452067/umfrage/gesamtschutzquote-der-asylbewerber-in-deutschland/. Accessed: 14. Sept. 2020.

Bundesamt für Migration und Flüchtlinge (BAMF). (2019b). Was heißt gute Bleibeperspektive? https://www.bamf.de/SharedDocs/FAQ/DE/IntegrationskurseAsylbewerber/001-bleibeperspektive.html. Accessed: 14. Sept. 2020.

Brandmeier, M. (2019). *Angepasstes und widerständiges Handeln in der Lebensführung geflüchteter Menschen. Handlungsfähigkeit im Verhältnis zu Anerkennung und (psycho-)sozialer Unterstützung in österreichischen Sammelunterkünften*. Weinheim: Beltz/Juventa.

Czollek, L.-C., Perko, G., Kaszner, C., & Czollek, M. (2019). *Praxishandbuch Social Justice und Diversity. Theorien, Training, Methoden, Übungen (Pädagogisches Training)* (2nd ed.). Weinheim: Juventa.

Dünnebacke, L.-M. (2018). Die Polarität der Gesellschaften. Transkulturelle Dialoge als Möglichkeit der Dekonstruktion von (Fremd-)Zuschreibungen. Sozialmagazin, 12, pp. 42–48. Weinheim: Beltz/Juventa.

Dünnebacke, L.-M. (2019). Soziale Arbeit in Kurdistan-Irak und Deutschland – ein Vergleich am Beispiel von Genderstrukturen. Empirische Zugänge im internationalen Dialog. Gender Studies – Interdisziplinäre Schriftenreihe zur Geschlechterforschung, 32, Hamburg: Verlag Dr. Kovac.

Eisnecker, P., & Schacht, D. (2016). Die Hälfte der Geflüchteten in Deutschland fand ihre erste Stelle über soziale Kontakte. Deutsches Institut für Wirtschaftsforschung (DIW), 83(35), pp. 757–764.

El-Mafaalani, A. (2012). *BildungsaufsteigerInnen aus benachteiligten Milieus. Habitustransformationen und soziale Mobilität bei Einheimischen und Türkischstämmigen.* Wiesbaden: Springer VS.

Filipp, S.-H. (1984). *Selbstkonzept-Forschung. Probleme, Befunde, Perspektiven* (2nd ed.). Stuttgart: Klett-Cotta.

Goffman, E. (1963). *Stigma. Notes on the management of spoiled identity.* New York: Simon & Schuster.

Habermas, J., & Luhmann, N. (1971). *Theorie der Gesellschaft oder Sozialtechnologie. Was leistet die Systemforschung?* Frankfurt a. M.: Suhrkamp.

Hollstein, T., Huber, L., & Schweppe, C. (2010). *Migration, Armut und Bewältigung. Eine fallrekonstruktive Studie.* Weinheim: Beltz/Juventa.

Johansson, S. (2016). Was wir über Flüchtlinge (nicht) wissen. Der wissenschaftliche Erkenntnisstand zur Lebenssituation von Flüchtlingen in Deutschland. Eine Expertise im Auftrag der Robert Bosch Stiftung und des SVR-Forschungsbereichs. https://www.bosch-stiftung.de/sites/default/files/publications/pdf_import/RBS_SVR_Expertise_Lebenssituation_Fluechtlinge.pdf. Accessed: 14. Sept. 2020.

Klassen, M. (2004). Was leisten Systemtheorien in der Sozialen Arbeit? Ein Vergleich der systemischen Ansätze von Niklas Luhmann und Mario Bunge. Veröffentlichte Dissertation [2003].

Krug, G., Drasch, K., & Jungbauer-Gans, M. (2019). The social stigma of unemployment: consequences of stigma consciousness on job search attitudes, behaviour and success. *Journal for Labour Market Research,* 53,11 Wiesbaden: Springer VS.

Laskowski, A. (2010). *Was den Menschen antreibt Entstehung und Beeinflussung des Selbstkonzeptes.* Frankfurt a. M.: Campus: Forschung.

Mae, M. (2014). Auf dem Weg zu einer transkulturellen Genderforschung. In: M. Mae & B. Saal, Britta (Eds.): *Transkulturelle Genderforschung. Ein Studienbuch zum Verhältnis von Kultur und Geschlecht.* 2nd edition, pp. 49–72. Wiesbaden: Springer VS.

Ministerium für Kinder, Familie, Flüchtlinge und Integration. (2018). Kabinett beschließt Stufenplan zur Entlastung der Kommunen. https://www.land.nrw/de/pressemitteilung/fluechtlingsminister-stamp-kabinett-beschliesst-asyl-stufenplan-zur-entlastung-der-. Accessed: 14. Sept. 2020.

Olk, T. (2017). Stigmatisierung. In D. K. Dieter, & I. Mielenz (Eds.), Wörterbuch Soziale Arbeit. Aufgaben, Praxisfelder, Begriffe und Methoden der Sozialarbeit und Sozialpädagogik, 8th edition. Weinheim: Beltz /Juventa.

Othman, A.-Y. (2013). Zwischen Kriegen und Globalisierung. Der Status der Frau im Nordirak (Südkurdistan). In S. Conermann (Ed.), *Bonner Islamstudien, 28.* Berlin: Verlag Dr. Brandt.

Plößer, M. (2013). Die Macht der (Geschlechter-)Norm. Überlegungen zur Bedeutung von Judith Butlers dekonstruktiver Gendertheorie für die Soziale Arbeit. In K.-P. Sabla & M. Plößer (Eds.), *Gendertheorien und Theorien Sozialer Arbeit Bezüge, Lücken und Herausforderungen* (pp. 199–216). Opladen: Barbara Budrich.

Täubig, V. (2009). *Totale Institution Asyl. Empirische Befunde zu alltäglichen Lebensführungen in der organisierten Desintegration.* Weinheim: Beltz/Juventa.

United Nations High Commissioner of Refugees (UNHCR). (2019). Convention and protocol Text of the 1951 Convention Relating to the Status of Refugees. https://cms.eme rgency.unhcr.org/documents/11982/55726/Convention+relating+to+the+Status+of+Ref ugees+%28signed+28+July+1951%2C+entered+into+force+22+April+1954%29+189+ UNTS+150+and+Protocol+relating+to+the+Status+of+Refugees+%28signed+31+Jan uary+1967%2C+entered+into+force+4+October+167%29+606+UNTS+267/0bf3248a- cfa8-4a60-864d-65cdfece1d47. Accessed: 12. Sept. 2020.

Walgenbach, K. (2007). Gender als interdependente Kategorie. In K. Walgenbach, G. Dietze, & A. Hornscheidt (Eds.), *Gender als interdependente Kategorie. Neue Perspektiven auf Intersektionalität, Diversität und Heterogenität* (pp. 23–64). Opladen: Barbara Budrich.

Walgenbach, K. (2011). Intersektionalität als Analyseparadigma kultureller und sozialer Ungleichheiten. In J. Bilstein, J. Ecarius, & E. Keiner (Eds.), *Kulturelle Differenzen und Globalisierung. Herausforderungen für Erziehung und Bildung* (pp. 113–132). Wiesbaden: Springer VS.

Printed by Printforce, United Kingdom